WHEN THE GIANT LIES DOWN

WHEN THE GIANT LIES DOWN

DICK & RUTH FOTH

VICTOR BOOKS

A DIVISION OF SCRIPTURE PRESS PUBLICATIONS INC.
USA CANADA ENGLAND

Editors: Jerry Yamamoto; Barbara Williams

Cover Design: Grace Chan Mallette

Library of Congress Cataloging-in-Publication Data

Foth, Dick.
   When the giant lies down / by Dick and Ruth Foth.
         p.   cm.
      ISBN 1-56476-388-9
      1. Interpersonal relations—Religious aspects—Christianity. 2. Christian life. 3. Leadership—Religious aspects—Christianity.
      I. Foth, Ruth. II. Title.
      BV4597.52.F68 1995
      248.4—dc20   94-37706
                                                              CIP

---

1 2 3 4 5 6 7 8 9 10 Printing / Year 99 98 97 96 95

Contents

A Word to the Reader

Writing a book together can be tough on a relationship, especially if the subject is *relationship*. Our greatest fear was putting another piece of writing out on the bookstand. But we were asked, and we considered. What you are about to read is the result.

This is *not* a marriage and family book. This is *not* a counselor's handbook. Neither is it a volume on leadership in the traditional sense.

Rather, it is a book of observations about why relationship is critical in today's world, how relationships are built, and where the leadership for that endeavor needs to come from. It has just a little "how to," but mostly "why not?"

The times in which we live challenge even the strongest person to look for answers that bring life to ourselves and those around us. We pray that our efforts here can help achieve that end in some small way.

Speaking of relationship, we could not have written this book alone. Our immediate family, Erica, Van and Alyson, Jenny, Susanna, and Chris, has been the joy of our lives and a great source of learning. We have a whole series of other families who have poured themselves into us and to whom we owe our deepest love and gratitude: The Blakeleys and the Foths; the Urbana congregation and the Bethany College gang; and finally, our most recent Washington, D.C. family.

A place to write is not always easy to find. Thank you to the McAlpines of Oakhurst and the Boyds of Kona, Hawaii. A special thanks to Sandy and Ann Guthrie of Newmill Farms near Perth, Scotland for their delightful hospitality, hot scones, and fresh raspberry preserves.

The impetus to imagine and complete a project like this was, at times, a critical issue. We are deeply indebted to the practical assistance and cheerleading of Bill and Nancy Carmichael. Thanks also to Senior Editor, Dave Horton of Victor Books for his consistent belief that the issues raised here were worthy of reflection in our day.

We hope this book helps you ask one question when you finish it, **"How can this happen where I live?"**

RICHARD AND RUTH BLAKELEY FOTH
Arlington, Virginia
May 1994

8

*"This will be a
sign to you: You
will find a baby
wrapped in
strips of cloth
and lying in a
manger."*

Luke 2:12

Chapter 1

In the Land of the Giants

A small body landed in the middle of my back without warning.

I was lying facedown on the living-room floor in a three-piece suit with the piled-up stresses of a hectic day just starting to drain away from me, when suddenly a tiny girlish body came out of nowhere. Then another body landed on my head. One landed on my legs. A fourth set of hands began tickling my ribs. Small bodies tangled with my large one—a squealing, squirming creature on the floor.

What a day it had been! Dozens of phone calls, three tough counseling sessions, one men's breakfast, one business lunch, one lengthy meeting with a building contractor, seven letters written, one stand-up staff meeting, ten waiting calls, a secretary left with only six of her ten questions answered. Then the race home for a brief dinner with the family . . . and a crammed evening just ahead.

With all that going on, it seemed entirely appropriate to

walk in the front door, toss my briefcase on the couch, and pitch forward spread-eagled on the carpet!

That the children would choose that moment to attack was equally appropriate from their point of view. Because little kids live in a mammoth landscape, they wander through a world of adult kneecaps and oversized chairs, all the while viewing the undersides of dining-room tables. That doesn't even take into account how they perceive an adult.

Adults are giants. A six-foot man is an awesome sight to a three-foot-high kid. In adult terms, that would be a twelve-foot man walking into a room of six-footers. The word *overwhelming* hardly begins to describe the feeling. But a magical thing happens when the big guy stretches out on the floor: The threat goes away. He looks absolutely different. He is accessible, touchable, open.

By physical dimensions alone, the parent in a toddler's home is God. Power. Authority. Direction. They are all wrapped up in that person. Those things don't change when the adult ends up on the floor, but they *feel* different. The power takes a relational shape. Horizontal is softer than vertical. Same size, weight, girth, but a different physical attitude. The position of the body quite naturally shifts from intimidation to invitation. Instead of preparing to fight ("drawing himself up to his full height"), he's preparing to play ("let's get down!"). In that moment, latent love, joy, and devotion explode in a tumbling, tussling dance on the carpet. It's not a social dance with complex steps and patterns. It is, rather, an interpretive dance with but two simple guidelines: *The adult must control his power, and everyone gets to play.*

Those moments become reference books in a child's library of experience. They are cataloged under "L" for "loving." Memorable loving is a touching, affirming, no-holds-barred collage of lives intertwined with each other bringing joy for its own sake.

For twenty minutes we went at it. A thirty-one-year-old

dad dissolving the pressures of a wild day with wilder play. And four children under the age of eight not caring a hoot for titles, schedules, or other lofty matters of business in the light of more important things, like jumping on the Giant.

Finally, the kids ran off in search of other adventures. I crawled over to the couch and eased myself onto it. Ruth, all this time, had been preparing dinner in the kitchen. She walked through the doorway in her apron, crossed the living room, and sat down on my lap. Putting her arms around me, she began to whisper sweet nothings.

Caught off guard, I grinned and asked, "Did you have a good day?"

She countered, "You played with the kids!"

"Well, they're *my* kids," I replied.

Whereupon she affected one of those let-me-explain-it-to-you-slowly-so-you-can-understand looks and said, "Oh, no! They're only *your* kids when you come home. They're *my* kids twenty-four hours a day. While you're off doing grand things, having business lunches, planning buildings, and meeting new people, I'm at home finding a two-year-old two houses over playing naked in the garden. And I have no idea where he put his clothes!"

For a reflective woman of few words, she was on a roll. Intrigued, I listened.

"When you come home and play with the kids, do you have any idea what that says to me?"

"No."

"What you're saying to me is that what I do counts. My world is important. That I'm a valuable person. What you are really doing, Dick, when you play with the kids, is you're loving *me!*"

I didn't know that, of course. I just thought I was knocking the kids into the couch.

Somewhere between playing with the children and listening to Ruth's practical discourse on the nature of relationship, I discovered something that day about *love, lead-*

ership, and *power*—those aspects of life and work that take on unique meaning when the Giant lies down.

Defining Love, Leadership, and Power

To better grasp the connection between these ideas, it might help to explain how they are addressed in this book. The definitions are not exotic or nuanced, simply practical.

Some years ago, a mentor of mine introduced me to this definition of love: *Love is the accurate estimate and the adequate supply of another person's need.* That compact characterization covers a lot of territory. It tells me three things:

> *(1) Love is the intentional exploration and discovery of another person's life.*
> *(2) Love is the assessment of the interests, desires, and needs of that person.*
> *(3) Love is the concerted effort to respond to that assessment in ways the other person will clearly recognize.*

Understanding that no definition of love is adequate, it is important to note that this one has historical and biblical roots. The Apostle John recorded it this way in the well-known text: "For God so loved the world that He gave His one and only Son, that whoever believes in Him shall not perish but have eternal life" (John 3:16).

When I apply it to myself today, it might read something like this: "For God so loved Richard Foth that He accurately estimated that he was a creep who needed to be reconciled to God and other people. God adequately provided reconciliation in the person of Jesus Christ so that Foth could live forever. Therefore, Foth knows he's loved."

Leadership as an idea is less straightforward because it takes on so many shapes and operates at so many different levels. In its simplest form, however, leadership can be defined as "the ability of one person to influence another person by presence, actions, and words." It's easy to see how that definition can be expanded in application to families, movements, and corporations.

Power simply means "the ability to act." We usually talk about power in measurable terms: Who holds it? How much do they have? How often is it used? How many ways is it abused?

Power also comes in several shapes: positional, relational, economic, and informational.

Positional power is official and structured, carrying with it corporate authority. It is transient. When the office is vacated, the authority is gone.

Relational power, on the other hand, is unofficial and unstructured, carrying with it personal influence. It is lasting. It lasts because it is a higher and more intimate connection that transcends office.

Nowhere is this truth seen more clearly than in Washington, D.C. Scores of men and women who may have held positions in previous administrations still live there. Their positions are gone, but in many cases their personal influence is still enormous. Why? Because, having built relationships, they still have access to the halls of power around the world.

Economic power can be connected to either a position (the control of assets) or a person (the creation of assets).

Informational power is similar in that position often gives access to strategic information, so an individual can make himself essential to an enterprise through personal insight and expertise.

Again, economic power can be lost quickly, and informational power is dependent on a whole range of things working just right—and staying that way. Position, economics, and information intersect one another in several ways, but they have a common flaw in that they can all disappear in a hurry.

In the long run, relational power transcends all of them

for one reason: it provides access. Real access to power of every kind comes only through relationship. And relationship is how life works. It is the essence of life. Therefore, when people become disenfranchised, left without persons who care about them or for them, life ceases to work. They are powerless. They have no access.

With that in mind, the essential theme of this book is about building relationships. Our thesis is that *the foundation of authentic living is quality relationships. Leadership and real power are only possible on that basis.*

One futher note. *Love* is not often used in this culture as a modifier to *leadership,* but since love is the deepest expression of relationship, we have chosen to use that word. To say that effective loving is effective leadership does not stretch the point. In fact, it makes the point exactly. Love, leadership, and power are related. When they can interact rightly with one another, the impact is profound.

A Human Model

In my young adult life and career, I had the good fortune of having several significant models for that interaction. One in particular comes to mind. I observed loving leadership in a father, grandfather, adventurer, entrepreneur, pioneer, board chairman, and pastor named Roy.

A strongly built man with hands calloused by his penchant for outdoor work, Roy Blakeley had a ready smile and a warm word for everyone he met. His deep, kindly voice had a welcoming, inclusive tone that bid strangers from the very young to the aged to come a little closer. His practice of meeting folks eye-to-eye meant he frequently hunkered down to speak with children. His husky chuckle was infectious and came from an attitude of not taking himself too seriously.

When we first met, he was thirty-four and I was eleven. He exuded hospitality. I was a nobody, yet he made me feel like somebody. Ten years later when I asked for his eldest daughter's hand in marriage, it was more of the same. Except this time I was afraid.

Pulling off Highway 99 near Modesto, in California's San Joaquin Valley, I made the phone call to his house. He amiably agreed to meet me in the parking lot of Stanislaus Elementary School on the Oakdale-Salida Highway.

When I clambered up beside him in his favorite old pickup truck that foggy afternoon, my heart was pounding. I had a dream and a problem. He could help me with both, if he wished.

With a foolish grin, I explained that I really loved his daughter. Coyly, he responded, "I can understand that. We kinda like her too." I asked to marry her, and with a smile and a pat on the back, he said he felt that could be arranged!

That was the dream. But the problem remained.

I explained haltingly that I was struggling with some facts and feelings. The facts were that my parents, great people whom I loved dearly, had been having marital difficulties. I didn't fully understand why or how they had gotten to that point. I'm not sure they fully understood either. But that December day, I was afraid that the things that had frayed the fabric of their relationship might be hereditary.

I tried to articulate those feelings in a number of different ways. He knew and appreciated my folks, and I could tell he liked me too. Finally, Roy Blakeley looked at me with a winsome smile and said, "Don't worry, Foth. Things'll work out. I trust you, and we'll trust God together."

That moment of affirming grace becomes more distinct and significant to me as I grow older. Years later, in my darkest days and greatest challenges, that simple verbal embrace would come back again and again. There was a very real sense in which that kindly man held my future in his hands, whether he realized it or not. He had maturity, wisdom, and power, but he did not flaunt them. He used them to unlock the door to my self-constructed cell and let me out into life.

In that moment I saw a loving leader. In an elementary school parking lot, of all places, the Giant lay down so I wouldn't have to be afraid.

A Divine Model

That human example, as profound as it was to me that afternoon, was only a reflection of a divine model. The songwriter in the nineteenth century would pen the words "O little town of Bethlehem, how still we see thee lie" as a reflection on a night that became the watershed of world history.

The Gospels tell the story in a marvelous way. They have animals and angels, light and sound. They have singing in the sky and crying in the stable. They have intrigue and treachery, human interest and divine intervention.

All that over a baby? It looked like just another peasant girl giving birth in an underdeveloped nation riddled by ethnic and religious rivalries and wearied by centuries of warfare. It appeared to be just another episode in the saga of a small country played as a pawn between superpowers. It seemed to be the birth of just one more male child into a fragmented Middle-Eastern society. But it was much more than that. The Bethlehem event struck at the core of what humans were designed to be.

It begins where we begin. In trauma and insecure circumstances, Jesus was born under a cloud of scandal among the Jewish people, who in the next 2,000 years would come to symbolize the entire range of human experiences. They would produce leaders to impact every aspect of culture—science, government, business, medicine, the arts, and more—only to suffer at the hands of others the horrors of multiple holocausts that boggle the imagination of rational minds.

In Bethlehem, God identified with human frailty, affirmed human value, and jump-started one more time what He had intended in Eden.

In that tiny Palestinian village, God put Himself directly into the mix to initiate a loving relationship with human beings. He invited access and response by coming in a most vulnerable manner. Part of the mystery of the Almighty melted away to reveal the touchable. Reconciliation was proffered with gurgles and dimpled fingers. It was the most nonthreatening act imaginable.

Bethlehem becomes a *statement* about the crucial need for relationship and reconciliation in an alienated world. It is a *model* for how a person who holds power can lead the way in that endeavor.

On that night God-the-Giant expressed His heart in a most radical manner: *He linked leadership and power in a way that humanity had never seen before. He used them to give birth to relationship.* It is worth noting that power expressed in gentle and controlled ways is often the mark of true leadership. To say it another way, self-control—power turned inward—is the basis for all quality relationships.

It would remain for Jesus to walk that idea out over the next thirty-three years. He would reach out to the lesser and the least. He would affirm children, saying "of such is the kingdom of heaven," in a society that discounted them. He would go out of His way to be inclusive. He would do things and say things that no one had ever done or said before. The people would see and hear, but few would understand . . . until later. In fact, the end of His earthly life would prove to be more dramatic than His beginning. But even at the point of death, He would be concerned for earthly relationships by making mutual provision for His mother and His best friend. What a strange, gentle Giant!

In the jargon of our day, we would say He specialized in connecting with dysfunctional people. Dysfunction is the operative word of our generation. It plagues every level and quarter of society. Billions of dollars are spent in

America annually to deal with that issue, and most often it has to do with dysfunction in relationships. The lack of ability to relate sometimes shows up in an alienation so intense that people take drastic measures in cities and villages across the land to protect themselves from random—and, in some cases, systematic—violence. Apart from this rather dramatic illustration, it's safe to say that we all have dysfunction and alienation somewhere in our lives.

The answer to alienation at every level is the Bethlehem principle: *intentionality in building relationships.* Leaders of all kinds have the potential to affect their colleagues and associates profoundly by taking this subject seriously. Making it "the first matter of business," vertically or laterally, could be revolutionary.

In the next few pages, we attempt quite simply to reflect on the framework and components that make for better relationships. They begin with inherent and intuitive need. We are designed for relationship, but we hesitate to reach out to others because of our *differences.* Once, however, we leapfrog those differences to identify our *samenesses*—whether by insight, training, or common experience—things begin to change. We become more willing to move toward one another.

The essential components of any relationship are lives shared in four ways: history-giving, affirmation, covenant, and dreaming. As we explore those arenas on our life journey, we discover that the deepest part of relationship is spiritual. Humans are distinctly more than cortical matter, motor-neurons, flesh, and bones. We are also spirit.

For now, however, we affirm with many who have gone before us that when God-the-Giant lay down at Bethlehem, everything changed. We don't have to be afraid anymore. If we don't have to be afraid of God, we can respond to Him. And if we don't need to fear God, we sure don't need to fear people. We can walk out of the cold and the dark away from our aloneness to the warmth of newly encouraged relationship. We can, but will we?

In reality, Bethlehem only sets the stage. Amazing things can happen when a leader catches the vision and leads the charge. An adult, a parent, a grandparent, a CEO, an elected official, an older friend. Someone like you. For when the powerful humble themselves, when authority becomes touchable, when relationship is nurtured with intentionality, it's Bethlehem all over again.

We will love the way we have been loved.

We will lead the way we have been led.

We will express power the way we have seen power expressed.

It began with Jesus in a stable. It continues with a leader in an old pickup truck or a young dad belly-down on a carpet. But in each unique expression, it is the Giant lying down. That singular act invites others into a loving relationship.

Intuitively, we know that relationships are what we're about. We may not always know how to create and build them well, but we know that we need others. Sometimes we have to be shocked into seeing how alone we really are. That recognition can become the place of beginnings.

Lie down on the floor, just like the Giant laid down.
Get down on the floor, like the Great God did at
Bethlehem-town.
Let me climb on your back, sit on your head,
Better than all the words you said;
Lie down on the floor, like the Giant laid down.

—*Ken Medema*
1993 Campus Life Midwinter Conference
Anaheim, California
Used with permission
Brier Patch Music/Ken Medema 1994

the persons of Wally Bennett and Ken Short.

Wally was a friend from earlier days in Illinois. An entrepreneur and real estate broker, he was a lover of people. I could walk and talk with him without pretense or posturing. He would listen, affirm, and encourage. Wally was relaxed and accepting.

Ken, on the other hand, was intense—not in a bad way, but in a focused way. He was in his seventies at that time and a retired missionary to Borneo, who was working with us in our development department. He had great stories of vision and faith to tell.

When I felt up against it and alone, I would call Ken and say, "Ken, tell me one of your stories." He would then proceed to spin a yarn about one of his incredible adventures in the South Pacific just after World War II. It would have impossibilities, intrigue, and the miraculous. That story would contain the antidote for my sense of isolation in some very practical way. The antidote was hope.

Hope most often shows up in the shape of other people—friends. Moses had Aaron and Hur. David had Jonathan. Jesus had Peter, James, and John, as well as the other apostles. Paul had Barnabas.

Friendship works for that reason. To sense another's presence and to hear a voice is reassuring. To this day I can hear the mellow tones of Wally and the excited expressions of Ken in my mind. Just to hear a familiar voice when we feel isolated is a comfort.

I learned that as a kid. A most insistent memory from my childhood is nighttime in the early '50s in Oakland, California. The Korean War was on. Americans were afraid of being A-bombed by the Soviet Union. I was a fifth-grader, and it was really dark in my room.

I would lie in my bed and sing every song I knew. Sing it out. Sing it loud. Keep away the night things. Don't move. Just sing.

Pretty soon I'd start calling my mom. "Mom. Mom! MOM!" You say, "Why didn't you just get out of bed and go find your mom?" Are you kidding? The guy under the bed would grab my ankle. And if he didn't get me, the one in the closet would. No way was I getting out of bed.

After what seemed forever, Mom would say, "What is it, Dick?"

I'd reply, "Aw, nothin'. I just wanted to know you were there."

I knew she was there. She was always there. Out of my bedroom, into the kitchen, through the swinging paneled door, past the central wall heater, into the living room. In that small house, built in the 1920s, she couldn't have been more than thirty feet away. A silly little distance in the day, but a universe away at night.

To hear that familiar voice was to touch something so deep and comforting in me that sleep followed quickly. Forty years later, Nyquil can't begin to compete with the protective presence and the steadying voice of another human being who cares. It reaches deeper than my aloneness and fear, connecting me to a more secure, life-giving world.

That need for another's presence goes beyond age, intellect, and training. It can be felt in the disturbing dark of a childhood night, but it can also be felt in the hammering havoc of nations at war.

During World War II, a phenomenon developed among crew members in Allied bombers flying sortie after sortie across the English Channel. Tail gunners, in particular, began to suffer fatigue, which in many cases led to nervous breakdowns. The pressure was constant and terrible. Night after night they would make their deadly raids into Germany, attempting to destroy the foundations of the Nazi Wehrmacht. Men would break under the strain.

Later, after recovery, the tail gunners' stories were similar: "I was under incredible stress. Always on guard. Anger and fear always present. The worst thing was having to maintain radio silence. I knew that my buddies were just a few yards away, but I couldn't talk to them or hear them. Sometimes I'd start hallucinating, seeing things that didn't exist. I'd start scraping little green men off my gun sights. I felt absolutely cut off and alone, and eventually it broke me."

The Original Problem

The erosive effects of being alone is a singular, common thread in the historical profile of humanity. One of the early Genesis statements says it all: "It is not good for the man to be alone" (2:18). True enough. Intuition tell₃ me this is so, and my experience confirms it. Aloneness has several different dimensions. A current author, writing of life in a home for the aged, elaborates: "The central problem of life . . . is, after all, only the universal problem of separateness: the original punishment, the ultimate vulnerability, the enemy of meaning."

The biblical story goes on to illustrate that statement. It recounts that among all the creatures in Eden "for Adam no suitable helper was found" (2:20). Subsequently, Eve was God's unique provision for Adam's aloneness, and he for hers. Each was designed for the other—trusting and vulnerable. They were given responsibilities and specific directives—not as monarchs of creation, but as accountable stewards. The fundamental connector between them was their common friendship and communication with God Himself.

All they had to do to be perfectly at peace and be productive was to listen well to God. In both the Old and New Testaments, to *listen* or to *hear* is the root for the idea of obedience. Obedience, however, came hard to these first earthlings. Choice entered the picture, and they chose otherwise. Breaking a covenant, they left God's presence, and the battle against aloneness began.

The Immediate Consequence

From then until now, the people of the earth have married, multiplied, and been buried, fighting for territory and power at every turn. Some have acknowledged The-God-Who-Overwhelms-The-Aloneness, but most have created other gods and have often claimed the job for themselves.

Self-rule seems to be a human penchant, regardless of its disabling consequences. And that thought brings the loneliness of leaders into bold relief. Just when I have achieved, made something of myself, and stood on the pinnacle, I find that there's precious little room for anyone else there. The competitive noises of those who desire my position are loud and real, but competition is not company. I am forced to play it close to the vest and mask my feelings. When I do that, loneliness grows. It often comes in stages and negates what I am designed for—one piece at a time.

The biblical story says we are designed to walk in the light, have control over our existence, be physically nurtured, and live together in harmony. When we go against that purpose, life itself winds down. We see how ultimate alienation comes in stages when we start playing a game of take away. Take away relationships from people. Take away food. Take away choice. Take away light. Without friends, without food, without choices, in the dark and cold, people break apart and die.

The Bible being true to life, is replete with stories that serve to illustrate such experiences: Joseph sold into slavery in Egypt by his own brothers; the Prophet Elijah running from Queen Jezebel into the desert—afraid for his life; Ruth, a single woman, struggling alone and impoverished in the workplace; David hiding in a cave from mad King Saul; the Gadarene demoniac chained in the tombs outside of town.

Amazingly, these stories don't have unhappy endings. Reading on, we discover that those people came close to God and found that the alone places were not lasting. Not the end of the line. When all was lost, they were found.

And the theme comes more clearly into focus: *Distance from others and God moves men and women toward dark-*

ness, impotence, and death. Intimacy with others and God
moves them toward light, power, and life.

The Essential Solution

Not far from Bethlehem, three decades later, God-the-Giant lay down again. Bethlehem had been an affirmation of humanity and intimacy and things held in common. Yet people's focus on differences, their tendency to personal failure, and their battle to be gods in their own kingdoms persisted. Something more had to be done. It was not enough to have a model—people needed a mediator.

What began in a Jewish stable, where creatures are born, nurtured, and live, was to end on a Roman cross, where people are tortured, derided, and killed.

The Giant would lie down one more time—this time to be brutalized and cut off from all relationships. The text suggests it took His willingness to endure temporary separation from His most intimate relationship to break the inward, downward spiral of alienation.

The subject of artists for hundreds of years, Jesus of Nazareth was nailed high and hard, impaled like an animal against a tree, sucking in air and pouring out blood. Flesh ripped, joints torn, suffocating under His own weight. This loving God/man, the Intimate One, sensed His Father turning away and screamed: "My God, My God, why have *You* forsaken Me?" (Matt. 27:46, italic added)

Jesus took the anguish of every person's aloneness to Himself and found the burden too great, the darkness too deep, the distance too much.

Nothing remained to protect Him. No one was there.

So death pounced.

Those few hours, years ago outside Jerusalem, the Great Aloneness ruled the night. Sometimes still the Great Aloneness rules *my* night. I am once again a ten-year-old calling for his mother in the night, a young executive caught up in a rushing world, a shaken adult heading for home in the wake of a natural disaster.

But the good news is there's more. Another chapter. A chapter about life and hope and a future. It's called the Resurrection. The incredible thought that a person could shatter the bonds of death—that ultimate aloneness—and burst into life again really does boggle the mind. But that's the good news of the Gospel story.

Jesus went into the grave alone, humiliated, burdened with our guilts. He came out of the grave three days later in triumph, as the Giant standing tall, having set the stage for us to be reconciled through His action to God, the Father, and to one another.

I particularly like the way the Apostle Paul said it some years later to some friends in the Greek party town of Corinth:

Therefore, if anyone is in Christ, he is a new creation; the old has gone, the new has come! All this is from God, who reconciled us to Himself through Christ and gave us the ministry of reconciliation. . . . God made Him who had no sin to be sin for us, so that in Him we might become the righteousness of God (2 Cor. 5:17-18, 21).

In Foth paraphrase, Jesus might have said, "Come here. I have a deal for you. Give me all the junk and glut of your life. All your failures, fleeting successes, lusts, manipulative behavior, and baloney. Let's trade. You give me all that stuff, and I'll give you My rightness, My power, My way of seeing things!"

It's almost too much to believe. If it's true, it gives me a chance to see things a whole new way. I can begin to think of the future. I can begin to think of others. I can begin to believe that relationships have a chance if I am willing to see people in a new way.

A Place to Begin

These walls I've built
so carefully
with my own hands
to defend myself
are locking me in
and shutting out
the light
and you
and . . . God.
How can I see to
open a window
or unlock a door
and find my way out?

—Ruth Foth

> *"On each side of
> the river stood
> the tree of life.
> . . . And the
> leaves of the tree
> are for the
> healing of the
> nations."*
>
> **Revelation 22:2**

Chapter 3

It's a Small World

S cotland dons its brightest tartan in May. Fields, from chartreuse to kelly green, and flowers—red-orange tulips cast among thousands of daffodils—clamor for one's attention. It is the proverbial quilted earth with stone-fence stitching. May in Perthshire is black-faced lambs, Shetland foals, scampering cotton-tails, and strutting cock pheasants.

This vibrant land of loch, lore, and legend has produced men as diverse as Sir Walter Scott, John Knox, Robbie Burns, David Livingstone, and the famed Blackwatch Regiment of the Queen's Own Highlanders.

Everyone in one sense has Scottish roots—not by nationality, but by experience. Everyone is a tartan of color, tradition, and people—things of laughter and life, desperation and death, mixed with "wannabes" and "If-onlys."

Sitting at a Scottish hearth on a misty May morning while listening to finches sing at the window of a 300-year-old stone farmhouse, we began writing this book—

our response to people's need for relationship. Enjoying a look at our Scottish side of the family in traditional plaids and woolen jumpers, we were challenged again by the fearsome differences and heartwarming similarities, which cause our deepest pain and greatest joy when woven together in the fabric of life. If the stone walls of that old house could talk, they would tell quite a story — a story affirming once again our need for one another.

The Grand Adventure

The human family is large and scattered. When I chance a look from my lonely vantage point, I am tentative, wary. Yet if I really explore, it becomes the richest of adventures.

If I'm careless in my looking, people's differences will put me off. But if I pace myself and don't prejudge, the samenesses in the family calls to me: "Look over here. You're near a treasure. Don't be in a hurry."

A dear friend of ours teaches design architecture to graduate students at a major Midwestern university. His specialty is master planning college campuses. One day as we talked over plans for our new campus design, I said, "Jim, how do you begin to know where to locate buildings?"

He grinned and said, "We do topographical studies first. But sometime during the process, often over a period of weeks, I will start walking the ground. It may be dozens of acres, but I will walk it early in the morning, at midday, and in the late afternoon. I'll walk it late at night. I'll survey it with my eyes over and over again from many different directions. Then pretty soon the land will start to talk to me, saying, 'Put a building here.' It doesn't happen unless you spend time. You can't rush to judgment."

And so it also is in walking the planet to discover the nature of the human family.

The Family Tree

Observe our biological family. Each member has his or her own history with anecdotes and tales sometimes grown into legend. Ruth's family has a 270-year-old oral tradition that involves the Maupin family, who came from England to colonial Virginia. During the voyage across the Atlantic in 1700, a fierce storm damaged their vessel, the *Nassau*. The vessel was taking on water, and despite the crew's efforts to repair the damage, it looked as if all would be lost.

The despairing captain asked Gabriel Maupin, a devout Huguenot, to offer prayer to God on their behalf. Miraculously the water level in the boat dropped, the crew's attempts to bail succeeded, and they made it safely to Yorktown. When they checked the ship's condition upon arrival, it was discovered that a large fish had wedged itself in the hole of the ship's keel. Myth? Tall tale? We later found this incident documented in the Virginia State Archives.

Enticed to further study of our family histories by such stories, Ruth and I took a trip to the British Isles, home to ancestors on three branches of our family tree. Our trek in the summer of 1989 took us by serendipity to Haddenham, England, a Cambridgeshire village sixty miles north of London.

While we overnighted in the area, Ruth said, "Let's check the phone listings for Presnells." I did, and there was one. I called. They were delighted to hear the name *Presnell* said with a beyond-the-Atlantic accent. We met that afternoon at the family-owned Three Kings Pub and had a grand time trying to make reasonable—or even fanciful—lineage connection.

In large part it came down to "William sure has a Presnell nose," or "There's that same red hair," or "You could be a young George Harvey!"

Family resemblances are passed on. Traits and tics, characteristics and quirks, mannerisms and moods. Sometimes they're learned, sometimes bred. And it's great fun to explore their roots.

One of the joys of tracing family history is being able to

feel something *now* by being connected to someone *then.* Oh, you take your chances. Over and over again, Irish folks with mischief in their eyes would ask knowingly: "Are ya sure ya wanta be diggin' around like that? Ya'r likely to find horse thieves!" Of course, we found no such thing. Well, perhaps a few cattle rustlers.

So it is with all families in world history. And what variety we find in people! In fact, we are so diverse that often at first glance it's hard to find anything in common on the surface.

A Snapshot

In the spring of 1972 at a conference in Sorrento, Italy, Ruth and I met Dr. Helmut Thielicke, a professor of dogmatics at the University of Hamburg. As a young man in the '40s, he had been a part of the Carl Goerdeler group, one of the coalitions attempting to confront the madness of Hitler. We had three extended occasions during that conference to sit with Dr. Thielicke and listen to stories, horrific and humorous, of Nazi Germany.

The first and most unique personal encounter with him was on the Amalfi Drive, west of Sorrento, heading toward the Isle of Capri. We were crammed into a Fiat 128 with our new friends, Margaret and Lyman Coleman, just out for a pleasant drive. Ahead we saw a car pulled off to the side of the road. It turned out to be Dr. and Mrs. Thielicke and their American interpreter. They were cheerful, friendly, and out of gas.

With a little ingenuity, we solved the problem, and all of us headed for the little fishing village of Positano. Once there, we made our way on foot down the winding cobbled streets toward the beach on the Tyrennean Sea. Small wooden fishing boats were pulled up on the rocky shoreline, as they had been for hundreds of years. Finding a quaint outdoor cafe, we sat down and ordered a sumptuous array of pasta dishes.

A grand storyteller, Dr. Thielicke entertained us during

our delightful meal with tales of his childhood, vignettes from his academic experience, and stories of great intensity from the Nazi years.

As we sat at the table, I remember thinking what a marvelous opportunity this was to sit with one of the great theologians and activists of our time. This compatriot of Dietrich Bonhoeffer had been saved from the hand of Hitler only by the protection of the Bishop of Stuttgart.

We were so different. I, a thirty-year-old American pastor from a low church tradition, and he, an aging German scholar from a high church tradition. The questions I had to deal with in my three decades were nothing compared to the range of issues he had grappled with during the '30s and '40s. He was a well-known scholar and professor of dogmatics. I was an unknown pastor with few recognizable accomplishments. We were so different.

But in those two hours, he drew me in. Beyond whatever might be considered a traditional Teutonic persona, this kindly gentleman with a fringe of white hair and resonant voice invited us to be friends. The way that he shared his story, speaking fondly of old acquaintances and telling hysterical anecdotes, was a mechanism that helped us leapfrog the years, language barriers, and ethnic understandings to land in his world.

He agreed to a taped interview for my radio program on a local CBS affiliate in Champaign-Urbana, Illinois. His response to my final question gave me a hint as to why I could feel so comfortable with him even though we came from different cultures, different times, and different places. Wrapping up the interview, I asked: "If you had one thing to say about God and man, Dr. Thielicke, what would it be?"

He paused momentarily, then in deep German-accented tones, he said, "Man is not valuable because he loves God. Man is valuable because God loves him." It was one of those *boy-I-wish-I'd-said-that* moments.

Later, in reading a compilation of Thielicke's sermons

on Genesis, *How the World Began,* I understood why he phrased it that way:

When we stop to consider where Jesus gained the power to love harlots, bullies, and ruffians, we find only one answer and that is that He is able to do this only because He saw through the filth and the crust of degeneration, because His eye caught the divine original which is hidden in every man—in every man.

The Design

Why does God love us? Because we're smart? Good-looking? Abound with native intelligence? Or perhaps because we implicitly and explicitly obey Him? Of course not! He loves us for the same reason we love our own children. We love them because they're ours. Whether they rebel, bond, run away, or snuggle, they're ours.

Humanity is God's intent, designed in God's image. That fact was meant to be a building block for relationship at any level. The problem comes in being able to see and appreciate that image. We cannot fully discover our own design until we become acquainted with the original.

In the '50s, one hot television program was the game show "I've Got a Secret." Selected guests tried to hide certain unique facts about themselves from the celebrity panel. If you stumped the panel, you won the game.

God, however, doesn't play that game. He *tells* His secrets. In fact, He does more than that; He tells *our* secrets. He tells us about the image that's covered up in His kids.

Everyone looks like God at the core. We have a spirit, intelligence, moral capability, and the ability to make choices. No difference exists between the landed aristocracy of Boston and the homeless of the same city—no difference despite being different colors, creeds, or characters. We are members of the same universal family.

The imprint shows up everywhere. The socialite in Houston. The baby in Chad. The pimp in Detroit. The student in Shanghai. The doctor in Stevanger. The alcoholic in Perth. The priest in Rio. Name the role, disease, dementia, location, or lifestyle. Though cast in a unique shape, each has the same needs.

We just need to take a step back and see with the Designer's eyes. Are we alike? More than we know. Take an Iowa farmer and his wife to Italy. When they've finished talking about schedule, kids, farm implements, techniques, struggles with land, conflicts with government, and dreams for tomorrow, do they have anything else in common? Yes, there's more. A deeper design exists.

The following story in Matthew's Gospel is illustrative:

> *Then the Pharisees went out and laid plans to trap Him in His words. They sent their disciples to Him along with the Herodians. "Teacher," they said, "we know You are a man of integrity and that You teach the way of God in accordance with the truth. You aren't swayed by men, because You pay no attention to who they are. Tell us then, what is Your opinion? Is it right to pay taxes to Caesar or not?" But Jesus, knowing their evil intent, said, "You hypocrites, why are you trying to trap Me? Show Me the coin used for paying the tax." They brought Him a denarius, and He asked them, "Whose portrait is this? And whose inscription?" "Caesar's," they replied. Then He said to them, "Give to Caesar what is Caesar's, and to God what is God's." When they heard this, they were amazed. So they left Him and went away (Matt. 22:15-22).*

The Pharisees went away amazed. And so did I at first reading. Why? Because I had no idea what this text really meant. In cross-referencing the language of the text, I discovered that the word for "image" in the Greek of Matthew 22:20 is the essential equivalent of "image" used in the Hebrew of Genesis 1:26.

Perhaps the scene played out something like this: They brought Jesus a coin. He held it up and said, "Whose image is this? Whose name is on this denarius?"

The Pharisees chorused, "Caesar's!"

Jesus tossed the coin in the dirt, pointed at it, and said, "Give unto Caesar what is Caesar's. A penny is the only thing he can put his image on! But," pointing directly at his accusers, "give unto God what is God's. You bear His image. He wants *you!*"

Jesus didn't respond to their point, but simply made His point, and they had nothing to say. By the flip of a coin, He took them back to basics.

Humanity is the expression of a creative God. For people to be seen as a mistake or a macroevolutionary fluke doesn't cut it. More than that, people are valuable for two reasons: God designed them, and God paid a price for them. If the value of an object is determined by the price that is paid for it—as any of us who has ever tried to sell a car or a home knows—then we really are valuable. I like the thought of the person who said, "I believe Jesus went to the cross to set the price on us so high, He could never be outbid."

A New Way of Seeing

If these statements about our image are true and our response to it is genuine, the implications for personal relationships are profound. C.S. Lewis in *The Weight of Glory* paints the picture this way:

There are no ordinary people. You have never talked to a mere mortal. Nations, cultures, arts, civilization—these are mortal, and their life is to ours as the life of a gnat, but it is immortals whom we joke with, work with, marry, snub, and exploit—immortal horrors or everlasting splendours.

The city of Calcutta drove this sentiment home to us. Ruth and I picked our way through stinking, littered streets on foot, a half mile from "the burning hills." The smell from bodies being cremated there in an open court hung heavy in the air, a sickly sweet reminder of lives for the most part lived in privation and pain. Our destination was a small hospice run by Mother Teresa.

We entered the nondescript building on the corner by an alley. The stench and heat gave way to a cool antiseptic feeling. The light was soft and diffuse in the low-ceilinged room. Pallets lined both sides of a concrete aisle. They held the dying, from the newborn to the ancient, being tended by workers moving quickly but silently among them.

A small chalkboard hanging by the door simply noted: Men—52; Women—71. The numbers changed daily, sometimes hourly. We stood in a peaceful anteroom to death, a place of dignity in a world of squalor, inhumanity, and pain. It was to Calcutta that Mother Teresa with her many coworkers came to live with the poorest of the poor. It was here that *homeless* showed its ugliest, diseased face. It was here that this young Albanian would commit herself to embrace the dying in a city choking on its own flesh. For people conceived, born, and raised to adulthood literally on the side of the road with no purpose, no direction, no means, and no hope, she would become an angel to bring a few hours or days of care to them before the end of their lives. It is here that Mother Teresa came to do *something beautiful for God*.

To keep back the tears was useless. We let them come. We made vows never to forget what we had seen and felt. And we heard her words once again, words from an old woman now. When asked how she could stand to retrieve the dying from Calcutta's streets every day, Mother Teresa simply said, "I'm not picking up the destitute and dying, I'm picking up Jesus." And we hear His echo, "When you do it to the least of these, you do it to Me."

It's not unusual to find humans in inhuman places, but to appreciate those people, we need to see clearly. We live in a pecking-order world where everything from *family lineage* to *appropriate neighborhood* are transient but powerful symbols to us. To be able to look beyond those transient symbols is the key to developing relationships. God sees that way. He moves into the uncharted territories of my own person and calls me out of hiding. Knowing the purposes for which He designed me, He comes hunting, not to hurt, but to heal. We are fallen and fragmented, exposed and insecure. He comes to help us gain our equilibrium and catch a vision for what can be.

We see God in Old Testament Eden, calling a frightened Adam out from behind the trees and again in New Testament Jericho getting Zaccheus down from one.

We, like Adam and Zaccheus, are afraid of God and drawn to Him at the same time. Instinctively, we keep our distance for any of 100 reasons, only to be discovered. We cover up, run away, scrunch down, close our eyes, lock the doors, and pile furniture against our doors. God appears in our rooms anyway. He shows up to tell us that we've missed the point. We are designed for more than running and hiding.

But hiding is our specialty. We mask our fears, run from confrontation, leap over renewing possibilities. We cover ourselves with the latest faddish fabrics and hide behind our schedules. But then He comes. He knows. We know that He knows. He opens His mouth and shouts, "Ollie, ollie, oxen free!"

The Zaccheus story in particular captures the power of looking beyond the external. This pint-sized swindler was up a tree and out on a limb. Of all the people in town to host a respected holy man for dinner, Zaccheus, a runner for the Romans, was the least likely. But Jesus affirmed Zaccheus by—of all things—inviting Himself over to the tax collector's home. And repentance happened. The search for Zaccheus was over. Greed became generosity, and everybody won.

So back to the family of humanity beyond my walls. It's really not so hard for me to believe that *I'm* made in the image of God. That's encouraging, even comforting. But my self-centeredness makes it tougher for me to accept the fact that *you* are. Nevertheless, I'm obligated to take you seriously. If I can see you as a mere accessory to my life, then I've no cause for great concern. But if indeed you bear God's imprint, everything changes. I am forced to acknowledge your presence. I come eyeball-to-eyeball with my pride and my prejudices. I must deal with God's intent.

Thielicke says it this way:

> But if [the image] is present in every human being, then I must take it into account, then I dare not react in fear or in hatred. . . . But rather learn to see them in the light of what they were created to be. . . . So for a moment at least, let us wipe away from our eyes the vision of human folly . . . and refresh ourselves with the vision of what God meant us men to be. . . . I believe it would be refreshment, if we were to expose ourselves to this breath of the Spirit in our history.

Looking for roots, our just-for-fun ancestral trek took us to the Three Kings Pub in Haddenham, England. But our for-real ancestral trek takes us straight to the King. We find out that we look like Him. Every one of us looks like Him. Now we are called to come to grips with that reality. If we really are one family, how do we discover our common roots? The next move is ours.

WHEN THE GIANT LIES DOWN

You sit as one apart—
So self-possessed, so sure, so unafraid.
I quickly judge you by mind's eye
and say, "So unlike me."
Hugging my fears, I sigh,
"No chance we could be friends."
But when you turn and look at me,
it's in your lonely gaze I see
that we are family.

—Ruth Foth

*"The man and
his wife were
both naked and
they felt no
shame."*

Genesis 2:25

Chapter 4

Naked Power

My mother's scream pierced the sultry Indian morning and brought the servants running in alarm.

In October of 1945, our family had been living in Kerala state less than a month. Staying in a house with concrete floors and barred windows, my older sister and I shared a room. That night we had shared it with another, rather unwelcome, guest.

Kerala lies on the southwest coast of India about eight degrees north of the equator. Giant ferns, hibiscus, and bougainvillea grow in rainbow profusion among hundreds of other varieties of plants. But the same climatic conditions that encourage that beauty encourage a similar range of insect and rodent life, from the rhinoceros beetle—the size of a half dollar—to the bandicoot, a rodent the size of a cat. And the food chain works there also, of course. Where rodents abound, snakes find easy prey.

Therefore, we shouldn't have been too surprised when a

cobra crawled into our bedroom through an unplugged drain hole in the base of the wall in the dark of that fall night. The snake had a simple growth task to perform. It was time to shed its skin. The floor at the head of my bed seemed as good a place as any. Fortunately for us, that was the one night during our first month in the country when neither Louanne nor I slipped out from under the heavy mosquito netting in the dark to find our way to the bathroom.

My mother, coming to wake us in the morning, screamed in response to what she thought was the snake. It turned out to be the skin. Two days later, around the corner of the house, the snake was found and killed. For the snake, the shedding of its skin was necessary to life. That metamorphic act, repeated again and again, allowed for its physical development. It could happen no other way.

Walk with me past our natural aversion to snakes and see the shedding of the snake's skin as a metaphor. The snake sheds its skin for the sake of expansion. In the same way, we need to make room for emotional and spiritual growth. The key to that aspect of human development — and, indeed, any kind of meaningful relationship — is the ability to self-disclose. Self-revelation helps rid us of the tight-fitting prejudices that inhibit growth and separate us from one another. Not to be able to be openhearted with another person is an impairment to one's personal life that is immeasurable.

The Potential Distortion

Admittedly, daytime television does not, on the surface, bode well for the case we attempt to make here. On a recent channel-surfing expedition, among the classic abbreviations — PBS, CNN, ABC, CBS, NBC, ESPN — the only designations that seemed to pop up were first names. Phil, Oprah, Montel, Sally, Maury, Jerry, and Geraldo — the titans of titillating television. If legitimate theater is the stage for societal expression, daytime television is the stage for self-disclosure taken to gruesome lengths.

Television producers and hosts have taken something natural—the need to share history, dreams, joy, and pain—and distorted it. What may have begun as a help becomes something grotesque. To the extent that self-disclosure is structured in that way, it becomes a cartoon. No direct connection to real life, it is not to be taken seriously. Thus to see it purveyed on television to make a dollar is to diminish the value of both the participants and the viewers.

Nevertheless, we would contend that neither distortion for monetary benefit nor traditional cultural conditioning negates the basic biblical model of humans needing to connect with each other, one-on-one, in a meaningful manner. And that activity presupposes self-revelation. Self-revelation is the singular foundation for initiating and nurturing relationships.

The Real Need

Psychologists for over 100 years have attempted to describe the essential needs of human beings. Several, including Abraham Maslow and his "hierarchy of needs," have brought significant truths to the forefront. Whether it is power, love, acceptance, or meaning that drives human beings to interact with one another in certain ways will forever be argued and evaluated.

Currently, some discussion is occurring among evangelical therapists about the validity of using the word "need" to describe the driving force in humans. The case is made that "need" is a word that should be used to characterize only our relationship with God. What we often call "needs," it is said, are really natural desires. For our purposes, we will use "need" in a limited sense.

The need for love and acceptance seems to lead the list when speaking of human relationships. To take that one step further, I would submit that *the need to be known*—or, more precisely, *the need to be known and still wanted*—should be given serious consideration as something of great import. If "know thyself" is a common and enduring axiom in the history of civilization, "let yourself be known by another" has to be the other side of the coin. In fact, it's doubtful that I *can* know myself adequately or accurately without reflection from others.

Our emotional and spiritual health is directly connected to this dynamic. In his book *The Transparent Self,* Sidney Jourard puts it this way:

[One can] only become well and stay relatively well when they come to know themselves through self-disclosure to another person. . . . Every maladjusted person is a person who has not made himself known to another human being and in consequence does not know himself.

The reason for the injunctions throughout the Old and New Testaments to "love one another" is not just that it reflects the character of God and His intent for humanity. An inherent need exists deep within us, recognized or not, to be known and still wanted by another human being.

Three thousand years ago, the psalmist captured the idea this way, when he declared the most critical level of need—the need to be known by God:

O Lord, You have searched me and You know me. You know when I sit and when I rise; You perceive my thoughts from afar. You discern my going out and my lying down; You are familiar with all my ways. Before a word is on my tongue, You know it completely, O Lord. . . .

Search me, O God, and know my heart; test me and know my anxious thoughts. See if there is any offensive way in me, and lead me in the way everlasting (Ps. 139:1-4, 23-24).

Sometimes I wish I had a Bible with inflection so that I could know the precise meaning. Is it "O Lord, *You* know me," or "You *know* me," or "You know *me.*" Whatever the emphasis or the tone, the fact is proclaimed in a way that leaves no question as to the focus of the statement: To be known by God is not intended as a threat but as a comfort—a confidence builder. Indeed, the assurance of God's love empowers us to reach out to others.

Setting the Stage

In the Bible, the stage for knowing another in depth is set early. A descriptive and insightful phrase is used right at the end of Genesis 2:25: "naked, and they felt no shame." Any mother, attempting to catch a naked two-year-old racing across the front yard toward that highway to adventure called the sidewalk, and listening to the shrieks of laughter and watching chubby legs pump for all they're worth, has heard the song of the soul set free. What is it about a child unclothed and running for daylight that expresses something deep within us? No doubt it's the age of innocence captured in a spontaneous act.

But this Genesis statement, coming at the culmination of the Creation account, implies the *other* relational dimension of nakedness that is not expressed in *innocence*, but in *knowledge*—two persons, committed and covenanted, reaching out to embrace each other for the purpose of expressing love, desire, need, and joy. Two becoming one—naked and not ashamed.

In the beginning, God spoke a world into existence and made a comment on it. He designed Adam to look like Himself. He breathed life into that man and instructed him to be a steward of his environment. Then He created another human of the same kind, but different in physical and emotional structure. God then said they were naked and not ashamed. What could this idea possibly imply?

The tendency of the reader may be to consider these words only in the context of the marriage bed. Certainly Genesis 2 is speaking to that experience. But it has to be saying something much more basic than that when taken with the rest of the text. The ramifications of biblical nakedness are far more than physical. Indeed, they may be essentially *not* physical. Words like "intimacy," "vulnerability," "transparency," and "openness" need to be used to express the broader understanding.

At the very least it means that people are designed for self-disclosure because God disclosed Himself. In fact, if we are made in God's likeness and designed for communion with Him, then the sharing of thoughts, feelings, pain, and joy is part of the intent. By revealing His character and His ways in the biblical story, God has already gone to great lengths to let us get next to Him. He calls us to respond to Him in the same way and ultimately to respond to one another. He does this by revealing Himself in Jesus Christ. He's saying, "If you want to know what I designed you for, how I want you to relate to one another, what kind of person you should and can be, look at Jesus."

The Apostle Paul picked up on that theme in a letter written to the Middle-Eastern church in a town called Colossae: "For God was pleased to have all His fullness dwell in [Jesus], and through Him to reconcile to Himself all things" (Col. 1:19-20). Jesus is the self-disclosure of the Father. His purpose is to offer us an opportunity for covenant. It takes us back to Genesis.

The idea of "covenant," used originally to describe God's arrangements with the man and woman in Eden, has much larger implications. Marriage may be the ultimate expression of covenant and closeness in human bonding, but it is not the only expression. Our lives are complex weavings of relationships at all kinds of levels. Each of those levels ultimately must incorporate the idea of self-disclosure or nakedness as its foundation.

Recognizing Resistance

By simple logic, if God exists and He created humanity, He knows all there is to know about people and their possibilities, strong and weak, good and bad. Had it been our choice as to whether He would know us so intimately, we would have resisted strongly for the obvious reasons—we are limited, flawed, myopic, greedy, and self-centered. We may also be adventuresome, visionary, compassionate, and generous, but it's the negatives that weigh us down, causing us to cover up and be defensive. It's instinctive.

Therefore, when someone knows all *about* us and is still *for* us, an amazing sense of trust and affection takes shape.

It is one thing to have no control over being known. It is quite another thing, however, to reveal voluntarily the real me as the primary move in beginning to build a lasting relationship. To expose at the right time and in the right way what is inside and underneath is metamorphosis— change for the sake of growth.

Those two activities, by their very nature, produce anxiety because change and growth are often painful experiences that move us into uncharted territory. Fear of the unknown is a natural response. We may not like to be anxious, but anxiousness is not the end of the world. If that anxiety can be nudged toward anticipation over time and in increments, then relationship becomes more viable.

Some people have fear about self-disclosure, because by nature they are not outgoing and they assume *outgoing* and *open* are synonyms. On the contrary, many gregarious, talkative people have only shallow relationships. They just have verbiage, too often just garbage bags full of words. They mask their essential need by talking. To them, silence and reflection can be disorienting, even threatening. I know. I'm a talker. One of my daughters caught it well when she laughingly said, "Dad, sometimes I think you just like the feel of words in your mouth."

But a dialogue on whether self-revelation is an extroverted or introverted thing should not derail the issue. In fact, it is true that some people can share their lives more easily than others, or, at least, with more people. But to stop there misses the point. This is not a question of personality style; it is a statement about design.

Understanding the Benefits
What are the benefits of self-disclosure?

Self-disclosure provides identification with the other person, a place to connect. When I begin talking about the broad range of persons, places, and events that have shaped my life, somewhere along the line, you and I are bound to find common ground. And when we do, the germ of relationship is planted. Again the biblical story leads the way. Jesus coming to Bethlehem as a baby illustrates God identifying with us in a most basic way . . . in our first trauma—birth.

A magazine centerfold caught my attention some years back. Since centerfold pictures are not commonplace in conservative, religious youth publications, this one caused a stir. Double page, four-color nude. Bloody, blue and purple, squalling. Umbilical cord still attached. A just-born, naked baby. And stamped across the bottom of the page in bold, block letters, it read "IMMANUEL—GOD WITH US."

It was scandalous! Oh, not the naked newborn. No, no, it was the idea that Almighty God would present Himself to us in *that* way. I mean, *I* was born *that* way. Didn't *He* come wrapped in swaddling clothes? And, of course, that's the point. God identifies with us and that gives us courage to attempt the same with others.

I will never forget, as an eleven-year-old kid, those days when my father—all 6'3" of him—would come home early from work. That was the opportunity to toss a football together in the street in front of our house. I loved his willingness to identify with me in that way.

Self-disclosure shows us again and again that we are much the same. We're at the very least the same in our clay-footedness and pain. We know some successes and victories, but we know many more sufferings in the struggle to run our own lives.

Speaking on a Mother's Day, I surprised myself by blurting out, just before the closing prayer, that I'd like the congregation to pray for my mom because she was alone. I'd never mentioned that circumstance to them before. Afterward, several older women came and hugged me. When I thanked them and asked, "Why are you doing this?" they each said pretty much the same thing, "You know, we don't always identify with your victories, but we really do empathize with your suffering."

The *samenesses*, give us a place to start. They establish a comfort level, arouse our curiosity, and drive us onward in pursuit of a relationship. Because of the significant investment of time and energy involved, few of us are willing to move ahead if there has been no connection or commonality established initially. The chances of finding things in common with another human being, however, in even the most remote part of this planet are great indeed.

On the other hand, our *differences* can be distressing, relational Everests, surmounted only with great difficulty. We are different in so many ways. Check out our physiology. That's the first thing we see and appraise when we meet a new person. I look at Arnold Schwarzenegger and say, "Of course God is a respecter of persons!" I could use every workout video from Jane Fonda's to Bodies by Jake, pumping iron 'til my pectorals met my neck, and I could not be Arnold. It's easy for us of ordinary physique to be intimidated by the rugged, the svelte, the tough, and the shapely. That's just for starters!

Family stock, educational advantage, wealth, ethnicity, travel, and range of experience—all can blend together in a conspiracy to create distance. Some folks, of course, use these factors to great social advantage. It is a natural thing to do. It may not be helpful, but it is natural. Wall building appears to come easier than bridge building.

How can we build relational bridges? In attempting to understand another person, we must embrace both the commonalities and the differences. The commonalities will encourage us; the differences will stretch us. The differences are certainly real, but they are as gnats to an elephant compared to the potential rewards of lifelong friendships.

The Starting Place

It may help to do a little analyzing before you begin. Who are your closest friends? The people to whom you can say anything and not be rejected out-of-hand? More than like-ly they are college classmates with whom you shared the challenging mix of dorm life, dreams, and your first adult decisions. Or one better, they are childhood friends. One of the joys of childhood friendships, continued into adult-hood, is that self-revelation takes place naturally through developmental years and shared rites of passage. The po-tential risk in disclosure simply doesn't exist. They've seen us, warts and all, already. Barring those kind of asso-ciations, however, we must move with intentionality to create the opening for vital and cohesive friendships.

This process does not have a tally board or a quota to fill. It is not natural for me to open myself deeply to doz-ens of people. I need only start with one. That, of course, is the only place I can begin. With one.

It takes time, some degree of comfort, and a reason. The two most important determinants of whether I will let down my natural defenses are the identity of the person I choose to speak with and the reason I wish to establish a relationship. If I find someone I think I would like to befriend, and if that person is willing to interact on the same level as I, I'm off to a good start. When that kind of dialogue occurs, prejudgments and misconceptions—the things that can cause distance—are forced into the open.

Self-disclosure may not always be a felt need, but for the sake of friendship, it is always a real need. Most often in life, learning begins with a felt need and moves to the real need. The need not to be lonely is certainly felt, but to leap to self-disclosure as part of the remedy is not one's first thought. In fact, our tendency is quite the opposite. We tend to withdraw further or lose ourselves in a noisy crowd. We follow our fearful feelings, and our feelings can send us in the wrong direction.

Pilots, of course, cannot afford to follow their feelings. Flying in clouds with no visual reference point poses great danger. They have to trust their instruments, which will tell them altitude above the earth and attitude in relation to the horizon. Self-disclosure is an instrument that will bring me safely home when correctly used.

Some years ago in a small group study based in the Old Testament Book of Ruth, we were doing some applicational exercises. The first chapter of Ruth is not exactly a grand adventure at Six Flags Great America. It's trauma with a capital "T." The entire fabric of Ruth's life had been ripped apart. She had been through high stress in a short period of time—famine in her homeland, the death of her husband, and a move to a foreign country.

In the course of the discussion, I raised the question: "What's one of the toughest things in your life that you've had to deal with?" I led the way, and one by one over the next forty-five minutes, the other seven participants shared difficult vignettes from their own lives.

One of my friends, who held a high-ranking position at a university, told of the summer between his senior year in high school and his freshman year in college when three of his best friends all died in separate, tragic accidents. The last incident occurred when my friend Jack and his buddy were swimming in the Mississippi River near St. Charles, Missouri. The young man was caught up in a strong current, and Jack went after him. Jack caught his friend and had him almost to the shore when his friend panicked, forcing Jack to release his grip. His boyhood friend was swept away in the rushing waters and drowned.

As he told his story, my usually self-controlled friend started to weep. The woman sitting next to him then turned to him and said something to the effect, "Jack, we come from very different backgrounds, and I've always felt beneath you. You dress well. You're articulate. You have a quality position at the university. And for some reason, I always thought you were snooty. Please forgive me. I was wrong." She then hugged him and said, "I love you."

In that fragile moment we were one. The power was almost tangible.

The Healing Place

Jourard speaks truth when he says:

Disclosure of one's being can be therapeutic. . . . To learn of another person's experiencing is to broaden and deepen dimensions of one's own experience. . . . Experience seems to be as transfusable as blood, and it can be as invigorating.

Those last two lines of the quotation—"Experience seems to be as transfusable as blood, and it can be as invigorating"—need to be read and reread. What a profound observation!

In the last thirty years, I've participated in hundreds of weekend retreats. In the most recent past, I've been in a number of conferences specifically for leaders—political, economic, scientific, medical, and ecclesiastical. In that part of the weekend when these folks, often as couples, stand to share incidents—past or present—with which they have struggled, something palpable happens in the room. The atmosphere takes on an empathy that is almost quantifiable. One can sense hearts reaching out and attitudes shifting, even as the speakers work through their stories. What seems to be weakness at first blush starts looking a great deal like strength.

What's most interesting is that this is the crowd that seemingly has it "together"—often people of intellectual prowess, communicative gifts, and wealth. But in that moment of self-disclosure, they grow. They become touchable, understandable, human beings. Moments before in my mind, they had only been people with assets of all kinds—something to give. Now they have opened themselves to both giving and receiving. More than that, my life has been enriched in a substantive way, because they have given me hope.

The giants were lying down, and in so doing, they were inviting me into their giant world. It seemed just like mine, only things were bigger and brighter and had more whistles. The dark places were about the same. Maybe even a little darker in spots. I felt comfortable there because I'd been invited in, not condescendingly as a servant, but as a colleague. It certainly changed the way I saw them.

Self-disclosure empowers both the speaker and the listener. Vulnerability and empowering are partners, though it might not feel that way at first. We have an innate sense that if we reveal something of ourselves to another, it will give the other person some leverage or control over us. As a matter of fact, that's true. It's true, that is, unless that person takes the information as a sacred trust and chooses to share a part of himself or herself, in which case, we're on common ground.

I choose to show you who I am, sometimes at risk to myself. But when I'm dealing with truth, truth in and of itself has power. So when James in his New Testament letter encourages people to confess faults (that is, tell the truth) to one another, he was not being masochistic, but realistic. He predicts that healing, empowering for wholeness, would result.

Self-disclosure can happen in lots of ways. I like to tell the story about Ruth's sister, Mary. She and her husband, Terry, have seven sons. At one point in their family history, all of the boys were under the age of fifteen! One day I made an unannounced visit to their home. As I entered the house, which was in only modest disarray, given seven boys—Mary looked at me through glazed eyes and said, "I'm sorry, Dick."

I said, "Why?"

She responded wearily, "I don't know. I'm just sorry!"

Well, we all have times of letting our guard down out of tiredness or burnout. But the kind of intentionality I suggest is caught in the game Mary and Terry used to play with their boys at bedtime. They called it "The Word Game," and it went like this: each boy would get a chance to choose a word, such as "horse," and Mary and Terry would both tell a story from their own childhoods about a horse. In that simple way, the children came to know their parents.

Our Place of Insight

Conferences in hotels can be killers. Registrations lost, misspellings on name tags, meeting rooms changed the night before, one towel and a soap short in the bathroom, and hamburgers that cost thirteen dollars apiece. A slow three-day death!

But not the one in the spring of 1972. With three kids farmed out to another family for two weeks, Ruth and I landed in Sorrento, Italy, for a conference called "Adventure of Living." Generous friends had paid our way, an act that would irrevocably change our lives. What we found were conferees almost twice our age, folks with adult children, people of means. Everything we weren't.

Right out of the chutes, day one, we were assigned to a small group—eight strangers trying to be nonchalant. Lyman Coleman led the groups. He was and is a pioneer in the small-group movement in the North American church. This mustached enthusiast exuded verve and joy and a certain kind of knowing. He knew this: *Given a chance and a little direction, strangers getting to know others in a relatively brief time is not an insurmountable task.*

Having been raised on a vertical theology—confession to God, but not to others—we were wary. We found, however, not a high-powered sensitivity group or an invasive confessional, but a fresh model for what it takes to build a relationship at any level in any place.

In the twenty years since, we have visited again and again the four steps suggested by Lyman as *the building-blocks of relationship: history-giving, affirmation, fellowship, and dreaming.* As a teaching tool, he presented the ideas as bases on a *relational baseball diamond.* With some modification and addition, we present those themes in the pages that follow with gratefulness.

History-giving lets us bring to each other information

and feelings about our personal journeys, along with the persons, places, and events that have shaped us (chap. 5).

Affirmation builds on that base. What we know of one another's pasts helps us understand how to love that other person more effectively. Positive language and actions nurture the relationship like nothing else can (chap. 6).

Fellowship places history-giving and affirmation in the context of a committed, ongoing relationship, which we have chosen to call *covenant* (chap. 7).

Dreaming builds on all the foregoing to give hope to the friendship. If shared history is the basis for a relationship, shared dreams energize and drive it (chap. 8).

Finally, we have chosen to look at the deepest part of our lives — *spirit*. That most intimate part of us that allows connection with God and one another. *Spirit* speaks to the center of our humanity, going beyond history, positive input, personal commitments, and hope for the future. It undergirds intellect and emotion. Although we make an attempt to illustrate what is implied in speaking of spirit, you will easily see that both words and pictures fail us. We can touch only the edges (chap. 9), but that is as it should be. With these places of self-disclosure as a guide, we must then make a choice (chap. 10).

The Critical Choice

Whatever else self-disclosure is, it is an attitude. When I take self-revelation as a given in social intercourse, a new sense of personal control affects my activities. By choosing to reveal my past with its shaping influences, my present with its joys and traumas, and my future with its four-masted dreams, I realize a sense of personal confidence that is achieved in no other way. The idea of giving myself away to get control of myself is an enigma, but it is right on the money. The congressman who says, "I'm a recovering alcoholic," is more in control than he's ever been.

On occasion someone will say, "I'm sorry, Dick, to take your time like this."

I often respond, "You can't be taking my time if I'm giving it to you. I want to do this." The offering of oneself is a freeing act for everyone involved.

Bracketed by the facts of history and a sense for the future as yet unrealized except in my imagination, I intentionally invite another person into my journey. No wonder that a new confidence, couching itself in words like "destiny," begins to show up.

What a grand design begins to surface—a design for love, leadership, and power. Nakedness is at the heart of it. Weakness, shame, and fear have to run away in the face of authentic nakedness. A new kind of power expressed in love is born.

The child running to the daylight, the lovers heading for the bedroom, the politician praying with a friend are all experiencing love and power. That kind of love and power begins with a decision to take a chance. In the seasons of living, self-disclosure is the springtime of the soul.

The rhythmic tapping at my study window draws me to it. White dogwood blossoms are framed there. Tugged by a gentle breeze, they encode a message on the pane: Spring has returned to the hills and valleys of northern Virginia.

On this May day, life's two necessities—change and growth—have shown up again. The blooms are back, but more of them. And the branch that they festoon is larger. I am once more reminded that the larger creation is a mirror to my own life, and a backyard can be a profound teacher. It has always been so.

When self-revelation becomes a natural expression of who I am, it's dogwood-blossom time again.

Playing dress-up again—just like a kid,
with clothes that don't fit,
shoes that are too big
and a hat that covers my eyes.

Just a harmless little disguise,
I think. But the longer it's worn,
not only does it hide me from you,
I no longer recognize myself.

—Ruth Foth

Chapter 5

The Gift I Bring: History

The sun's rays like warm fingers gently closed my eyes as I struggled to concentrate on the industrial revolution in North America.

The final semester of my senior year at Fremont High in Oakland, California, was winding down. Just three months and I, with thirty-seven of my classmates, would be entering U.C. Berkeley for the college adventure!

History was such a bore. Just get past Mr. Smith's U.S. history class, and I'd be home free. His closing words jolted me awake: "Your last assignment is a fifteen-page paper on a personality from nineteenth-century America. Someone who made a difference, pioneered a geographic region, or led the government."

Not wanting to think too creatively, I asked his advice after class. I was willing to write about a pioneer, but no one as well known as, say, Kit Carson or John Fremont. He suggested, "Why not do something with one of my cestors. One of the original mountain men—Jedediah Smith?"

Sounded good to me. I pursued the topic, detailing the life and deeds of this tough, adventuresome man who died in 1830 on the Sante Fe Trail at the hands of the Apaches. By the time I was finished, I was hooked. That began, for me, a real love affair with history.

I believe it happened because I knew Mr. Smith. He had some of ol' Jedediah's blood in him. History came alive. History-with-skin-on-it all of a sudden became very interesting.

No question that history can be dull, and for good reasons. It may be taught without sufficient context. It may be fact-centered rather than theme-centered. Whatever the cause, kids often struggle with the subject, not because they lack curiosity about life, but because they don't have enough personal history to get a sense for the larger view.

When we are young, we stand in valleys. Everything around is larger than we are. As we mature, we stand taller and on higher places. Perspective grows.

Reading history speeds up that process and broadens one's view immeasurably. We come to find that generations before us have thought great thoughts and dreamed great dreams. More than that, they stood on the shoulders of those who went before *them*.

History doesn't just take us *back*, it moves us *up*. We look backward to go upward, and in so doing, our appreciation for life with all of its ebbs and flows is intensified. That's why history fleshed out is the foundation for relationship. To reflect on our own past and be willing to invite another to take a look is a logical place to start.

Of course, the first place to gain such appreciation is by looking at my own history—as far back as I can research—with keen interest.

In 1976, I watched television's first real miniseries, *Roots*. The drama, historical reality, and good acting all merged to hit me right between the eyes. One episode was particularly touching. Kunta Kinte, the abducted African prince, had been brought to Annapolis, Maryland, and sold. As time passed, he and his wife had a daughter named Kizzie. A white plantation owner raped her when she was a young woman. A son was born to that forced union, and later on Kizzie named him Chicken George because he liked gamecock fighting.

Years went by, and Kizzie fell in love with an American-born slave named Sam, but ultimately she decided against marriage. An adult by then, Chicken George asked her why she had broken the relationship. I will never forget her reply: "Chicken George, honey, Sam 'merican, not African. He don' know Africa. An' if'n you don' know wheah you comes from, you cain' know wheah you a'goin'!"

To reflect on my own history is a most significant part of the journey. To do so with the help of others and to help them reflect is a marvelous experience. It is the keystone in any relationship.

The Nature of History-giving

We quickly discover two things when we start dealing with personal history: Everybody has one and each story is unique. In a fiercely competitive world, that's good news. The arena of my history does not need to be another place to compete. One person's past is not better than another's. They are simply different.

What is simply is. What's done is done. I cannot change anything. How I treat my history makes all the difference, of course. I can ignore it—the ultimate desecration of myself. Bash it—a most futile endeavor. Reflect on it—begin understanding myself. Offer it—the first step in creating a friendship.

To have a part of my life in which no competition is required or even possible is almost too good to be true. This truth is not about highbrow or lowbrow, educated or uneducated, cosmopolitan or provincial. Breeding and good stock are pointless references here. This is one person's story—a true and vibrant account of a life lived out in the apparent caprice of time and place. It is replete with people, places, and events, coming to confluence in one human being. Sorrows and joys, triumphs and tragedies are found in that house called my mind. It is the house of remembrances with rooms and closets and porches. And apart from this particular moment, every single thought or experience there is historical.

I am a walking, talking history book. Unique. Complex. A compilation of chapters with footnotes. A locked diary to which I alone hold the key. You may not read me at your will, only at mine.

Some chapters seem bland or trite, others unnervingly passionate. One is written in the language of first love, another in the blood of fractious battles and grievous misunderstanding. The parts have sequence to them, but there are thoughts behind words and motifs behind experiences. Neither does my book detail life lived on a single plane. Rather, it has length and depth and breadth.

If you take the time to stand beside me, we may, at some point, decide to read each other aloud. Reader's theater in two-part harmony. Antiphonal history. *War and Peace. Romeo and Juliet. Heidi. Beauty and the Beast. Crime and Punishment. Genesis. The Lion, the Witch, and the Wardrobe. The Prince. Christy. The Scarlet Letter. The Velveteen Rabbit.* And much, much more. We have bits and pieces of all these themes in us, but in variety of order, emphasis, and arrangement. Some persons' histories are more dramatic than others, but none is more important than another's. It is who I am and always will be. The only way I will change it is by writing new chapters.

As we talk to each other, an equality emerges. We sense ourselves growing in confidence. In the marketplace one often hears phrases like, "They're playing by a different set of rules" or "It's not a level playing field." In the exchange of personal history notes, however, those complaints cannot apply. We pay each other in the currency of our lives. Our remembrances and perceptions are legal tender.

And so it is that personal history, authentically presented, is a gift to any relationship. Conversely, that story withheld can negatively impact everything from friendship to the marriage bed. How can one person befriend or love another effectively if the things that have shaped personality, worldview, attitudes, responses, and dreams are not explored? I am a composite of the relationships and experiences of my past. I may or may not like my history, but I and those around me will continually have to deal with its effect on my life. In reality, my past and my perceptions of it are all I have to give you. Today is only a starting place, and tomorrow remains to be seen. We bring our pasts to this relationship as gifts to exchange.

Yet talking about personal background is hard work. If our past has been difficult, we want to forget it and get on with life. Even if our past has been pleasurable, it still takes energy to discuss it.

Many of us don't wish to discuss our growing-up years, possibly because of associated pain, either self-inflicted or imposed by others. We need to learn to distinguish between those experiences and identify some responses to them. For example, the biblical story is clear about the remedy for self-caused pain. The Apostle John says it this way: "If we confess our sins, He is faithful and just and will forgive us our sins and purify us from all unrighteousness" (1 John 1:9). Sin, by definition, is "missing the mark." Those failures confessed to God are freely forgiven and forgotten. It is unnecessary to relate those historic poor choices or wrong actions to other people in order to have quality relationships. That is not to say that events resulting from poor choices should *never* be told to another, but confessing every sordid thing you've ever done in front of a crowd is rarely, if ever, a help.

Another category—injury that has been caused by other

persons or circumstances—needs always to be recognized and sometimes to be communicated. I am not a therapist, but dealing with my own fifty-two-year history has made me face the fact that a goodly amount of healing can come from simply *recognizing* the historic components that have shaped my attitudes, angle on life, and responses. I don't even have to make a value judgment. Just acknowledge that it *was* and *is*. Like my stuttering.

From my earliest days, I can remember having difficulty speaking fluidly. Public reading in school was an ongoing trauma. Any structured situation that required verbal skill caused me great stress because I was a stutterer. Just like other diseases, though stuttering is nontransmittable, it makes people nervous and uncomfortable. If one can't speak clearly, the implication is that he's stupid.

Over and over again, I would dread going to science class in junior high school because reading aloud would also be practiced there. Up one row and down the other. Student after student, each reading a paragraph aloud. The closer it came to my turn, the more tense and frightened I would become. Something in me wanted to scream, "I can't do this! I *won't* do this!" I wanted to run out of the room, but I knew I'd have to come back. Science quickly lost its appeal for me.

I did all kinds of things to overcome my verbal problem. I created mechanical gestures, trigger phrases, and a range of other devices to help me through the minefield of communication. Two things that I did to compensate, without knowing it at the time, were to tell jokes and participate in drama. The speech therapist had diagnosed my problem: "You think in paragraphs, Dick, and struggle with speaking in sentences." Consequently, the words would seem to jam up behind my teeth. If I could memorize phrases and pace myself, it allowed me to speak without distortion.

I memorized jokes, which made me socially acceptable. Folks like people who make them laugh. And the memorization of lines for a dramatic character allowed me to get out of myself and, at the same time, have a popular identity. Years later, in a graduate school speech class, I would be given high marks for "the effective use of the dramatic pause." In reality, I was only pausing for an extra beat or two to gather my thoughts in order to deliver the next sentence without stuttering!

Today my style of public speaking quite naturally reflects my attempts to compensate for speech difficulties in those growing-up years. Humor, poetry, and storytelling are an integral part of how I communicate. They are not there because I planned it. They are there as an appropriate remedy to a young boy's fear. What began as problem-solving has become part of my style and personality.

I stutter now only when I am extremely tired or under tremendous pressure. Reflecting on that healing process, however, makes it clear that part of the solution to my stuttering problem was acknowledging the condition in front of my friends and even learning to poke fun at myself. Once I was able to tell my friends what they already knew about me, I was released to relax and work through this social challenge.

At a different level, some of the history that shapes us is not traumatic, just incomprehensible to others. When our four children were small, I was constantly correcting their table manners with such comments as "Sit up straight. Chew with your mouth closed. Don't reach in front of people!" In her quiet way, Ruth would chastise me for being too obsessive: "Why do you do that, Dick? You're compulsive about table manners."

I'd mumble some response like "I don't know, it just comes from somewhere inside."

Then came the trip to my boyhood home in South India in the spring of 1973. Conoor in the Blue Mountains was home to Hebron School, where I attended classes as a youngster.

I couldn't wait to introduce Ruth to the Bird's Nest (my dorm room as a five-year-old), Dinkytown (the dirt hillside racecourse for matchbox metal cars), and *marble poochies* (quarter-size millipedes found under leaves in the adjacent forest). But the first thing we received was an invitation to 4 o'clock tea at the school. We walked into the dining room to find British school girls in starched blue pinafores sitting up straight at long tables, chewing with their mouths closed, and saying politely, "Please pass the wau-tuh."

The light went on as Ruth exclaimed, "That's it! That's where you got all that manners business!"

In the larger view, some would say that personal history—genetics, environment, and events—traps us. Locks us in with no way out. If that is true, then the good news from God—we can be healed, whole, and have a future because of Jesus—isn't worth a snap of our fingers. All is lost. We're stuck. Dead-ended. Hopeless. The remedy, of course, is found in the manner in which we *deal* with our personal past. History does not have to *trap* us, but it certainly does *shape* us. As we talk to each other, we can see much more clearly those shaping influences.

As you read this page, no doubt a dozen things come to mind as shaping influences in your growing-up years—powerful personalities, traumatic events, family gatherings, dinner-table routines, and so on. They all contribute to the person you are at this very moment.

Looking at the Shaping Influences

If reflecting on personal history is vital to growing a relationship, what can help trigger that process? Just to say "Tell me about your life" may not get us very far. It's difficult to sit down and just talk about our histories with no frame of reference. One of the mechanisms that Lyman Coleman uses in his workshops is the "childhood family table." In groups of four to six, individuals will draw their childhood, family dinner table as they remember it. The family members are placed in their accustomed positions around the dinner table, and if coloring crayons are available, they are given colors denoting the way the artist sees them. The family is then described to the other group members by the artist, including the underlying feelings and atmosphere that were part of the table setting.

Over the last twenty years in retreat settings, I have participated in this exercise dozens of times, always with meaningful results. Time and again, the most obvious result is simply that no two tables are ever alike.

At a military dependents' retreat in the Bavarian Alps, one eighteen-year-old youth approached me and said, "Which of my eighteen tables would you like me to draw? I've moved every year of my life."

At a high school camp in the Tennessee hills, a pastor's son drew three small rectangles in a semicircle with a square on the open side of the semicircle. Pointing at the rectangles, he said, "That's my Dad, my Mom in the middle, and me on the other end. And that's," pointing at the square, "Walter Cronkite [then anchor for CBS News]. All of my growing up days it was three TV trays in front of the TV."

I have a friend in his upper seventies who still communicates powerfully with teenagers. He, like so many other public speakers, has a life theme. My friend, Ed, can start anywhere in the Bible—the map section, the chronologies of the Old Testament, the general epistles—and end with this declaration: "Because of Jesus Christ, I am somebody."

At a youth retreat where Ed and I were both speaking, we drew our childhood family tables. He drew one extremely long table with about fourteen place settings and an adjacent table for two. Dotted lines connected the two tables. We saw his table and exclaimed, "Good grief, Ed, you came from a huge family!"

"Not exactly," he responded. "I was raised in an orphanage in Rhode Island." He then went on to explain that the circles drawn at each place setting were bowls of oatmeal. "Every day, every week, every month, every year, for all of our growing-up days, our house parents fed us bowls of oatmeal. We had meat once a year at Thanksgiving. On the other hand," he continued, "our house parents had meat dishes every day. Those dotted lines I drew between the tables are hate lines. We hated them because they said to us, in effect, 'You're worth one bowl of oatmeal.' "

Ed then described how an older lady down the street had invited him to a church service as a young teenager. That night the speaker explained that Jesus loved all of His creations and would make them *somebody* if they would follow Him. Ed made the decision that night and excitedly ran home to tell his house parents. They responded by beating him. He was not allowed to return to church for two years.

"I can still remember going to my room that night," Ed said, "kneeling beside my bed with blood streaming down my face, and saying 'Jesus, I don't know why they did this to me, but I love You, because You're making me *somebody*.' "

And all of a sudden, I understood why Ed spoke the way he spoke and what connected him so powerfully with struggling teenagers. He had been there.

On occasion people will say, "I can't remember my childhood family table." With today's fragmenting family structure, that response is more and more common. I'll not soon forget the man who looked across the table at me at a conference and said, "I'm embarrassed to say I can't remember the shape of my table." Pausing a moment, he said quietly, "Perhaps it's because when I grew up I went to forty different schools. My father was an alcoholic. He kept drinking up the rent money, and we would be evicted each time." Quite softly he continued, "I've never told anyone this before because I thought they might think less of me."

His candor moved each of us around the table quite deeply. I responded by saying, "My respect for you just went up 1,000 percent. To see who you are and what you have accomplished, having come out of that formidable circumstance, is a testimony to the grace of God and your tenacity." It was an exquisite moment.

Another time at a teachers' conference, a lady approached me and said, "I can't remember my table because I never ate at home. I grew up with my father in the Bronx, and for every meal he would send me to the corner Automat to get something out of the canteen, and I would eat there by myself."

The simple mechanism of sketching one's childhood family table gives us a jumping-off place for reflection on circumstances that are extremely meaningful in our lives. Even the absence of a family table is quite significant.

It is absolutely amazing how many things we can find in common once we start talking. Simple things like childhood games. At a retreat outside Manassas, Virginia, a few years ago I asked the question, "What did you do for fun as a kid?" People started calling out activities, games, and sports like red rover, kick-the-can, hide-and-seek, ice skating, all kinds of team sports, dirt clod fights, BB gun wars, and finally one attractive blonde lady in the front row raised her hand and said, "I rode pigs."

The room exploded in laughter, and I asked, "You what?"

She repeated with a grin, "I rode pigs."

"Where were you raised?" I asked.

"On a farm in Iowa," she answered.

"How in the world do you ride a pig?" I asked.

"You just stand up on the trough and wait for a big sow to come up and feed," she explained. "You pick one that hasn't had a recent litter, because she'd be mean. Then you just jump on her back, grab her ears, hang on, and off you go."

By the time she finished her description, we were convulsing with laughter, and as an impromptu thought, I asked, "Did anyone else here ever ride a pig?" Five other people shyly raised their hands. They came out of the pig-riding closet.

Since that day at many retreats, I've asked whether there are pig riders present, and virtually without exception, there will be some. There is a fraternity of Swine-Sitters Anonymous scattered far and wide through the suburbs and cities of this land. When they deal with this historic truth, they find great release and joy! So do the rest of us when we hear it described.

In a marriage relationship, the sharing of personal history is critical because each partner brings lots of baggage along. It is not the earthshaking questions about the universe that plague us in our marriages; it's the pieces of history that we expect to be reenacted by our spouse, like "Why doesn't she bake apple pies the way Mom used to?" or "Why isn't he the fix-it man like my dad?" We don't squabble over the fact of Christmas. We get into it over "Do we open presents on Christmas Eve or Christmas morning?" It's amazing the heat that can be generated over a twelve-hour time difference.

One day as I walked past the kitchen, I noticed Ruth and our four children coloring Easter eggs. I poked my head in and asked, "What are you doing?"

She said, "We're coloring Easter eggs. We're going to hide them in the bushes and have fun finding them."

With pontifical authority, I said, "You can't do that."

"Why not?" she asked.

"Because it's an ancient Egyptian fertility rite," I countered. "The goddess Osiris, springtime, pagan stuff."

She gave me a look that spoke volumes and muttered, "I don't know about all that. We're just putting color on these eggs. We're going to hide them and find them. It's fun."

I said again, "You can't do that. It's an old pagan ritual."

She looked at me, this time with fire in her eyes, and said, "Our children know the difference between the resurrection of Jesus and the Easter bunny. And besides, my grandparents and parents did this with us when we were growing up, and we loved it. Are you saying that my grandparents and parents are pagan, Dick?"

Instantly, seeing the precipice, I retreated, saying, "Oh, no! I didn't have that in mind at all." I then left to go to work, and they hunted eggs. They had more fun.

Once again, I saw the challenge: *Try to understand rather than prejudge personal history.* Categories are convenient. Prejudgments and prejudices are easy ways to go. They are defense mechanisms that will kill us. But the answer is to walk away from those useless, listless devices and walk into adventure. By sharing my past, I meet it head-on and make it a full partner for my future.

The Supernatural Model

The model for using history-giving as a basis for relationship is The Story—God's account of His dealings with individuals and groups over thousands of years. It is the self-revealing narrative of His aggressive, redemptive behavior on our behalf. The difficult is detailed, as well as the glorious. The bad as well as the good. The Story as a whole—Old and New Testaments—is an encouragement toward trust, because knowledge feeds trust.

The range of human frustration, degradation, passion, and joy is slathered like an oil-paint rainbow on the biblical canvas. We find it all—from innocence to incest, from the idyllic to the insane. Families ripped apart, cultures clashing, nations at war. The greatest despair and the grandest hope just a few pages apart. It's all there with God right in the middle—waiting, watching, acting.

When we see how God deals with people who hate Him, run from Him, and run to Him, we are encouraged to trust Him with our lives. When that kind of history is shared, respect and trust—the two critical components in any relationship—are engendered. Not only are these components nurtured, but structure is also created by which I'm able to love effectively. That is to say, once I can understand what you've been through, how your dreams have been shaped, and what's important in your life, I can better know how and where to love you the way you need to be loved.

Because covenant and the command to love one another loom so large in both the Old and New Testaments, it stands to reason that God Himself would lead the way in showing how good loving is initiated. Simple. Just tell the folks where you've been, what you've done, and what's happened to you.

If love is "the accurate estimate and the adequate supply of another person's need," knowledge of another's history plays a huge part in specifying the format by which that person can recognize loving acts. It is easily seen by looking at how God loves. That is, one of the reasons God can love us absolutely is that He knows our history absolutely.

Virtually anything and everything in our past can play some part in our approach to the people around us. From the smallest nuance to the greatest trauma, history can leave an indelible impression on human personality. Some issues can be disregarded; others have to be dealt with. But to the degree that all of them are recognized over a period of time for what they are—shaping influences in one's life—they will bring a depth of richness to any relationship, which can be achieved by no other means.

My history is not dead. Every day I breathe, it lives. Thus, for me to mine that vast resource in order to build a relationship is one of the wisest things I can ever do. When both of us can see our pasts as gifts to each other, it can be Christmas every day.

Getting to know you is taking a trip to the past—
short pants, grinning, freckled face, English accent and all.
Since our first meeting, thirty years ago,
I'm still discovering your childhood face.

—Ruth Foth

*"Pleasant words
are a honey-
comb, sweet to
the soul and
healing to the
bones."*

Proverbs 16:24

Chapter 6

The Attitude I Choose: Affirming

J ust how did you conquer your stuttering?" the speech pathologist asked with some interest. I had just finished speaking at a five-hour seminar in the course of which I had commented on the stuttering difficulties I had, which persisted through young adulthood.

"Three things set me free," I answered. "First, I believe Jesus had a unique part in fixing my thought and speech processes. Second, I would sit in my college dorm room and read everything from the newspaper to Hamlet out loud. I found that if I read in elongated syllables I could do so without an impediment. And third, persons affirming me in spite of my dilemma were a tremendous asset."

Affirmation from others is an incredibly freeing act. It is water in the desert. Amazing things grow in and around that pure stream. I was doing all I could to help myself overcome my speaking struggles, but I could go only so far. Ruth's affirmation changed that profoundly.

I'll never forget a particular date our senior year in college. I was feeling extremely insecure and opted to give her a way out if she so desired. We were driving along West Cliff Drive in Santa Cruz, California, and I said to her, "Probably you w-w-wouldn't want to keep going with me because I can't t-t-talk well."

She looked at me with a grin and said "Oh, really? I hadn't noticed." Having spent time with me, she knew where affirmation needed to land.

As I share my history with others, I quite naturally am allowing those persons into my world. They come to know my parents and grandparents, my siblings and friends. They become acquainted with my teachers and coaches. Old girlfriends. Neighborhood bullies. Childhood pets. And on it goes.

Knowing those parts of my experience gives others a basis for speaking into my life positively, challenging or confirming, but always nourishing my perception of myself. People who continually emphasize my value as a human being are using that four-dollar word—affirmation.

Affirmation unlocks death's door and lets me out into life. Very simply, it is me telling you how I see you in qualitative terms. On the one hand, I can affirm you for what you do, but that means you have to keep performing. On the other hand, when I affirm you just for who you are and what you mean to me, that goes beyond.

To say "I like you" is one of the most profound accolades we can give someone. Deep down we all want to believe that we are likable, worth loving, valuable to another human being.

In a friendship, authentic affirmation is built on history-giving. I know where to speak into your life because I understand where you've come from and what you've come through.

The kind of acceptance that is reflected in the way friends talk with each other is an expression of a common understanding. As we invite each other to go exploring—

take a guided tour really—into the terrain of our pasts, we tell the other person who we really are. Sometimes it's an adventure along a historic family river or a hike up an extinct academic volcano. We might even do some spiritual spelunking. When that happens, we open ourselves to the possibility of vibrant, here-and-now affirmation.

The question really is "How do we go about affirming another person effectively?" Is it words, actions, or time? The answer of course is yes to all three of the foregoing. Perhaps by using the first chapter of Philippians, we can illustrate how affirmation fits into a developing relationship.

Philippians has been dubbed by some "The Epistle of Joy." Paul wrote from prison to his friends in Philippi to let them know how *he's* doing and to encourage them in what *they're* doing. It's clear in the letter that Paul had a real affection for these people because of their history together and their belief in his mission.

After the usual greetings, Paul wrote a preamble to begin the letter that captured the essence of his dreams for them and his gratefulness for the ongoing mutual relationship that they enjoyed. Verses 3 through 11 read this way:

I thank my God every time I remember you. In all my prayers for all of you, I always pray with joy because of your partnership in the Gospel from the first day until now, being confident of this, that He who began a good work in you will carry it on to completion until the day of Christ Jesus.

It is right for me to feel this way about all of you, since I have you in my heart; for whether I am in chains or defending and confirming the Gospel, all of you share in God's grace with me. God can testify how I long for all of you with the affection of Christ Jesus.

And this is my prayer: that your love may abound more and more in knowledge and depth of insight, so that you may be able to discern what is best and may be pure and blameless until the day of Christ, filled with the fruit of righteousness that comes through Jesus Christ—to the glory and praise of God.

Four key approaches to affirmation surface here. The

first is *words to God about you*. Call it thankfulness, call it prayer, but essentially, the pray-er is saying, "I think you're so valuable that I will bring your name and your need before my Heavenly Father." Paul says, "In all my prayers for all of you, I always pray with joy" (Phil. 1:4). Too often "I'll pray for you" is a throwaway line, a comma in the middle of a relational sentence. In fact, to pray for another is to commend him or her to the Person who cares the most.

Some years ago in a church service with a couple of hundred people in attendance, I took time to ask for prayer needs. Jim, a young man in the second row on the right side, raised his hand and said, "I'd like to pray for Paul Todd." Paul Todd was forty years his senior, a veteran tank commander under George Patton during the Second World War. The spearhead division had been involved in some of the most intense fighting of the war, all the way from North Africa to Germany. In the last year of the war, Paul had been severely wounded when he was blown out of his tank. He still suffered the pain of that period of his life, both physically and emotionally. Paul couldn't speak in any detail about the war without weeping.

After Jim said, "I'd like us to pray for Paul Todd," I responded, "Fine. Is he in the hospital again?"

Jim said, "No."

"Is he struggling emotionally?" I asked.

He answered, "I don't think so."

I continued, "Well, you know he's battled with depression on occasion. Do you think that's what he's dealing with now?"

Jim said, "I don't think so."

Finally, noting that I was having this conversation in front of 200 people, I blurted out, "Well, Jim, why do you want to pray for him?"

Whereupon, he flashed me an innocent smile and said, "Oh, I just like him."

That caught me completely off guard. Didn't he know that you only pray for people who are sick and hurting, not for people you like? What would happen if we prayed for people just because we liked them?

Second, affirmation is expressed in *words to you about you*. Or better yet, words to a third party that get back to you. We need to hear over and over again that we are valued and valuable. Something fundamental happens when another person says, "Just being around you is a joy," or "When you come into the room, something exciting happens," or "You have a great smile." Our essential being is validated.

It works with children. Research shows that similar accolades toward small children create healthy children who grow up to be productive. It works in marriage when mates address positive attributes in the other person. In our day-to-day search for meaning, we need for others to tell us who we are. I didn't marry Ruth Blakeley for her to tell me what I'm not. I know what I'm not. I desperately need for her to tell me who I am.

The Apostle Paul affirmed the Philippians with these phrases: "I thank my God every time I remember you" and "how I long for all of you with the affection of Christ Jesus" (Phil. 1:3, 8). His constant reflection about them and his desire to be with them says it all.

On occasion, the right words can result in powerful responses right on the spot. Some years ago, I was part of a small-group training process. We had shared history for several hours in the morning. After lunch, we reconvened and began a session centered on affirmation. The instruction to the groups of six was to arrange five chairs in a horseshoe and put the sixth chair at the open end of the horseshoe. Each person would take a turn sitting in that sixth chair. On the basis of what we had learned about one another, we would go around the horseshoe and individually affirm that person in terms of a color, a quality, or an animal. We might say, "I see you as bright orange—

warm, enthusiastic, glowing," or "I see you as a gentle person, sensitive to the needs to others," or "I see you as a bear—strong, protective, willing to fight for your own." With this in mind, we started.

One of the participants was a twenty-eight-year-old church education director from a Roman Catholic parish in a neighboring state. She had received a negative critique at the end of her first year of service.

During the morning she complained about the activities, the day, and the process itself, chain-smoking all the while.

When it came to her turn, she hesitantly sat in the chair. A nineteen-year-old girl from Rockford, Illinois, then looked across the horseshoe at her and said, "I see you as the color of your dress (a silky dress with a rust, orange, and brown pattern in it), because it reminds me of a fire in the fireplace at my home in Rockford. I'd like to take you to my home on a snowy winter's night and sit with you in front of the fire, drinking hot chocolate and eating popcorn, just to get to know you."

After the girl finished her brief monologue, the education director took the cigarette out of her mouth and put it on the tile floor. Looking straight at the young girl, she said, "Say that again."

The girl repeated it with simplicity and warmth. By the time she finished the last sentence, tears were streaming down the education director's face as she said, "No one in my whole life has ever asked me to sit in front of a fire for an evening just to get to know me." The woman was transformed before our eyes. She was a different person the rest of the day. Why? Affirmation unlocks my door and lets me out.

Third, *positive actions toward you* are affirming. Romans 5:8 captures it succinctly. "But God demonstrates His own love for us in this: While we were still sinners, Christ died for us." It doesn't get any better than that. The sacrifice of one person for another is the highest accolade.

In 1964, at Wheaton College Graduate School, Ruth and I were working night and day on my thesis, a topic relating to Latin America. My adviser was Dr. Lois LeBar, a petite, insightful woman, one of the top three professors in my student career. Her compassion for people was real; her knowledge of her discipline was profound.

One afternoon, she asked how my research was coming. I was at her home, working on a lesson plan for a college class that she was observing. I told her that I needed more primary resource material and I was scrambling to find it.

She asked, "Are you going to the Urbana InterVarsity Conference at Christmastime? Lots of people from Latin America will be there."

I told her that I wasn't, because I didn't have the $100 it would take for Ruth and me to be able to go for the week (not much money now, but a fortune for a graduate student then!).

She didn't say anything, but rose to her feet and walked toward her bedroom in the back of the house. She returned three minutes later, took my hand and pressed five new twenty-dollar bills into it.

Then, she looked up at me and said, "This is important. You and Ruth need to go."

That action, the investment of $100 in the lives of two young people, changed our whole world. We later returned to Urbana and lived there for over eleven years. The conference we went to radically altered how we saw ourselves, our mission, and others.

Some actions are not so dramatic. The friend who helps you on moving day, the neighbor who bakes a pie, the child who gives you a crayon drawing that looks like a miniature Picasso are all expressions of affirmation.

Fourth, affirmation comes in the shape of *actions toward your world.* Our world consists of the place or places we spend large and meaningful chunks of our lives. When you show an interest in my line of work or workplace, that ascribes meaning to what I do.

Only eight weeks earlier, Ruth and I had moved to Urbana, Illinois, to begin pastoring twelve university students. I was green as a gourd and still stuttering some. I hardly knew where to start. Then he showed up. A sage at forty years old, he was fifteen years older than I. Paul McGarvey, a football coach at a large high school, was enthusiastic, fun-loving, and real.

Most significant of all for me, Paul took me seriously as a person and as a pastor. We ended up being together for nine years before he moved on, recruited to bigger and better things. To this day, we count Paul and his wife, Eileen, as two of our dearest friends.

When we built the first building, we had only twenty-five people. So Paul and I dug ditches, made light fixtures, sealed basement walls with tar, and painted ceilings with great gusto and little skill! I will never forget talking football, motivational techniques, and theology until early in the morning on several chilly autumn nights. He was with me when it counted. He supported our sense of calling. He followed my youthful, ignorant leadership. He was saying my world counted.

When we began a preschool, Eileen pioneered it, working from daylight to dark. She was a buoyant, positive personality in a small and growing place. When Paul and Eileen left, the church was home to hundreds, and the preschool home to scores. But for Ruth and me, their impact was not in the numbers. It was in our worldview, our attitudes, our appreciation for Jesus.

Paul and Eileen McGarvey had loved not only us, but more than that, they had loved our world.

Those loving acts are magnified when they come at an important moment in a person's life. Like when I played the lead role of John Proctor in Arthur Miller's *The Crucible*.

Our high school cast had practiced for six weeks — several hours every night. It was a magnificent challenge for a stutterer like me. My dad told me that he would be there the second night. We had only two nights of performance.

When the curtain came down to wild cheers and applause on that first night, I was thrilled. But, the clincher came when my dad suddenly appeared backstage to hug me and say, "I couldn't stay away." I will never forget that moment.

Positive interest in another person's world will rarely be taken as intrusion. Rather, it will be read as it is intended—a sincere interest in a friend's life and work.

Yet when all of the affirming words and actions are completed, there still remain situations in which conflict arises in any quality relationship. At that point, we must be prepared to deal just as authentically with confrontation. Confrontation needs to balance affirmation. On the relational scale, *balance*, for most of us, can be achieved by landing somewhere in the range of 95-percent affirmation and 5-percent confrontation. Affirmation creates the context in which productive confrontation can occur.

David Augsburger's treatise on dealing with conflict, *Caring Enough to Confront*, is an extremely helpful synopsis on confrontational style. Assuming that conflict itself is neutral, he suggests that there are five ways to deal with conflict. Our reactions move it toward a positive or negative.

The first method is *I'll get you*. I'm right, you're wrong, and I'm gonna get you. All of us have tried this brontosaurus approach on occasion. We may win the skirmish, but we never help the relationship.

The second way is *I'll give in*. You're right, I'm wrong, and I'll accommodate you. This stance is too often accompanied by a pout, an affected smile, or just a cowering silence. Accommodation, however, brings no character or richness to the relationship. It is, in fact, a subtle kind of lying about how one really feels.

The third method is *I'll get out*. Running from conflict

is natural. But again resolution rarely results, unless, of course, someone distances himself or herself to cool off and then returns to interact rationally. I heard an explanation for this option during a missionary retreat in Cartagena, Colombia, in the summer of 1990. One of the participants told the story of a couple who was being honored in a southern church for seventy-five years of married life. During an interview, the couple, in their nineties, was asked the inevitable question, "How did your marriage last this long?"

The old gentleman replied, "Well, Ma and me agreed when we was first married that if we got into an argument, I'd go out and sit on the porch until we cooled off. Then I'd go back in, and we'd talk it through. I guess it's lasted this long because of all that great outdoor livin'!"

The fourth way to deal with conflict is *compromise*. You come part way, and I'll come part way. Getting better.

However, Augsburger indicates that the best and most biblical way to deal with conflict is to *affirm the person and confront the issue*. In a day when people are perceived as the issue, the idea that a person might be affirmed and the issue confronted really is good news.

In the eighth chapter of John, we find a poignant example of Jesus' approaching a person in just that way. The Pharisees, the religious ultraconservatives, found an adulteress and brought her to Jesus. They, of course, wanted to trap Jesus. Meanwhile, she was just a pawn in their chess game. Some men would use her—one more time—this time in the name of righteousness.

The adulteress was brought to the temple courts where a crowd was gathered. The Pharisees challenged Jesus with these words: "In the Law Moses commanded us to stone such women. Now what do You say?" (v. 5) No easy answer here, just a trap. The text picks up the story:

But Jesus bent down and started to write on the ground with His finger. When they kept on questioning Him, He straightened up and said to them, "If any one of you is without sin, let him be the first to throw a stone at her." Again He stooped down and wrote on the ground.

*At this, those who heard began to go away one at a time, the older
ones first, until only Jesus was left, with the woman still standing
there. Jesus straightened up and asked her, "Woman, where are they?
Has no one condemned you?"
"No one, sir," she said.
"Then neither do I condemn you," Jesus declared. "Go now and
leave your life of sin" (vv. 6-11).*

We don't know what Jesus wrote in the dirt. We do
know that He challenged her accusers and His assailants
quite simply: "Fellas, let the one of you who has never
missed the mark or crossed over the line, throw the first
rock." In my imagination I can hear the sound of rocks
being dropped, not thrown, as the eldest—the eldest had
more sins—to the youngest melted into the crowd. When
Jesus stood up the second time, the only sinless person
who could be standing with the woman *was* standing
with the woman.

I can see Jesus reach over and lift her chin, so she has to
look directly at Him, while asking, "Who accuses you?"

I can see her glance back over her left shoulder and
then her right to find no religious types, just an irregular
semicircle of rocks on the ground. Turning back to Him,
she says, "Nobody."

I can see Him smiling, as He responds, "Me neither. Go
and don't do that anymore." If we were to read the affirmation behind those eyes, Jesus could have been saying,
"I designed you to be a great lady and that's not the kind
of thing great ladies do." He was affirming the person
while confronting the issue.

When we consider Jesus' life as a whole, it tells the
same story. At Bethlehem God assumed a human form. He
in effect said, "I designed people to be good. I will show
them how it's done." He affirmed humanness, spending
thirty-three years living among us—eating, sleeping, con-
versing, laughing, suffering, and dealing with social ills
and personal hurts.

But on one spring Friday with the thunder rolling and

the earth heaving, He confronted the damaging issues of my life and impaled them on a Roman cross. Then, bursting out of the tomb on Resurrection morning, Jesus confronted the greatest issue of all—death—and overwhelmed it with life.

My Heavenly Father affirms me always, and as part of that process, He confronts my issues day after day. The stage was set at Bethlehem. The drama was acted out over three decades through the life of Jesus in a strife-torn land, ending in a cruel death at the hands of political and religious interest groups. But the grand finale on Resurrection morning brought down the house.

E. Stanley Jones, the sainted missionary-statesman from India, has called Jesus *The Divine Yes*. That shouted *Yes* echoes between the shepherd's cave in Bethlehem and the burial cave of Joseph of Arimathea, Jesus' benefactor. It flies in the face of those who say, "This could never be." It unlocks death's door and lets me out into the light. He lets me know that I count.

Now it's my turn to try unlocking some doors.

The Attitude I Choose: Affirming

Your words,
used powerfully,
can either bind my soul
or set me free.

The picture of myself
I often see,
is the image in your mirror,
held up to me.

—Ruth Foth

> *"I now establish
> my covenant
> with you and
> with your
> descendants
> after you."*
>
> *Genesis 9:9*

Chapter 7

The Place I Stand: Covenanting

I'm on you like ugly on an ape, Foth." Hardly Oxford English, but certainly the explosive heartfelt expression of a friend committed to my well-being.

"I'm making a covenant with you during this time," he continued, "to check in with you systematically, and to be available when you need me, and I expect you to tell me the truth about how you're doing." In the face of an extremely trying circumstance, I needed that friend to stake out territory in my life. I did not need judicious, intellectual dialogue. What was needed here was passionate commitment.

The idea of covenant showed up early in the Story. The transaction in Eden was shaped in the form of a treaty arrangement commonly used hundreds of years before Christ. It was straightforward. A preamble. Terms of the agreement: Blessings if the terms were kept; consequences if the agreement was violated.

The rest of the Story is full of covenant agreements after

Adam, even though he and his mate fouled up. Noah, Abraham, Moses, David—they all were the beneficiaries of covenants with God.

Two kinds of covenants were used. One kind had stipulations by both parties. The other was unilateral: One party stipulated the terms, and the other party accepted or rejected those terms, but could not change them. In either case, the idea of covenant was positive and meaningful.

We all need to have someone—besides God—covenant with us. And we need that covenant on at least three levels: time, tenacity, and truth-telling.

Covenant of Time

If my personal history is the gift I bring to any relationship, then my personal time is the covenant I make to grow it. In Western culture, quality, focused time is like the rain forest—it's rapidly disappearing. The damage done to the relational environment can hardly be overestimated.

The friend who readily agrees to meet over dinner, the child who wants to play, the mate who wants to ride in the country have one desire in common: time. If spending time together is such a critical component of our lives, why isn't there enough to go around? Too many times we find ourselves overcommitted to the urgent, while the important takes second place. Time is the most slippery thing in the world. It gets away from us. We must guard it judiciously.

One evening I arrived home after counseling hurting people all day. Just bushed, I had no emotional energy left. I sat down in our easy chair and tried to escape children and wife by hiding behind the newspaper. With a quizzical look on her face, Ruth prodded me, "Dick, why is it that you give the quality, prime time of your day to people you hardly know, and we get only the leftovers?" Good question. It led me to do some rethinking of how I spent the most valuable commodity of the day.

The reasoning goes something like this: God's method of communication is Incarnation—in-the-flesh, personal presence. Since God is capable of doing things any way He wants, why did He send Jesus? Why not just emblazon "Come to My house" in the Aurora Borealis of the northern skies and let the message flash for 2,000 years, slowly letting new disciples carry the good news to the southern hemisphere? Why put flesh on the words? Probably because humans believe presence more strongly than they believe words. Your presence has the potential for touching all my senses while your voice or writing touches only my hearing or sight. Giving me your presence automatically gives me your time.

Time spent together has a way of bonding a friendship like nothing else. Part of that has to do with common experience: to go adventuring, see a sunrise, ride the waves, sit in front of a fire. When we spend time together, we share experience. One moment. One opportunity. Forever gained or lost.

One day I was waxing eloquent on the values of quality time. Hearing that lofty monologue, Ruth went right to the heart of it when she interrupted, "Forget the quality. Give me quantity. The quality will take care of itself."

Theologians are fond of noting that the power of the Holy Spirit infused the early church after the Day of Pentecost in such a way that the message of Jesus Christ was spread around the Mediterranean basin and beyond in a handful of years. It is worth observing, however, that Acts 2:42 and the following verses indicate Jesus' disciples met together daily from house to house. In modern terminology we would call that a support network. What they found was a kind of interaction and empowering that developed because they spent time at it, had common history, worked at self-disclosure, and had a common goal. They could have had history and the intent to self-disclose, but never moved ahead because they didn't spend enough time together.

Some years ago, a tragic event occurred in a friend's family. I worked with them night and day to the point of my own exhaustion. Finally, I called another friend in Pasadena, Texas, Allen Groff. He is "Tex" to me. I said, "Tex, can I come and see you for two or three days, just to be there and walk on the beach with you?"

He immediately responded in the affirmative.

I flew out to meet him. As we drove toward Galveston from his home, I started to pour out my frustration, anger, and pain over my inability to see something significant happening out of tragedy. I felt like a failure. I was angry at God and angry at myself. In the middle of that oral explosion, I began to weep. Not a prolific crier by nature, I couldn't hold back the tears as they coursed down my cheeks onto my shirt.

Tex didn't say a thing. He just reached out and put a hand on my knee and kept driving. It was ten or fifteen minutes before I was able to speak. As I looked up and started to say something, I noticed Tex. Tears were streaming down *his* cheeks onto *his* shirt. And it was all right. He was my friend. That was what I needed. My friend without words.

It is significant to me that when Jesus went away, He said, "I will ask the Father, and He will give you another Counselor to be *with* you forever—the Spirit of truth" (John 14:16, italics added). And again, "Surely I will be *with* you always, to the very end of the age" (Matt. 28:20, italics added). Although the kingdom of God is illustrated through miracles and other kinds of high drama, the focus of Jesus' relationship with His followers is summarized in His ongoing presence with them. If I can be assured of your availability, we can have hope for all other aspects of our relationship.

Even in the penning of these thoughts, the idea of time-nurturing-relationship seems so elementary as to be hardly worth mentioning. But we have been seduced in this sound-bite society into believing that most, if not all, things are immediate, transistorized, and Daytimer defined.

Quality relationships are not that way, are they? They are grown over time, through pain, and under scheduling conflicts, demanding that choices be made. Time becomes oxygen for meaningful friendships, marriages, and business relationships. In the same way that oxygen-rich blood nurtures every cell in your body, minute by minute, day in and day out, year after year, so time freely given infuses friendships with life-giving nutrients. It has no substitute. The critical issue then becomes perseverance — the willingness to stick with it.

Covenant of Tenacity

Not long ago I was asked what one quality was most helpful among individuals in organizational teamwork. I mentally went through my list of preferred competencies — vision, communication skills, flexibility, listening, commitment to growth, and so on. Finally, I said, "Follow-through. Staying with it."

In a flippant society, where narcissism wages war with commitment, the very idea of tenacity in covenant with another person in friendship, marriage, or business takes it on the chin.

Today's marital scene is often too weak an example to use as a model. Wrong expectations, unknown histories, and unclear goals can all contribute to the failure of marriage. One of the reasons that marriages fail is that they are set up to do so. A relationship entered with the thought "If it doesn't work, I'll change partners" is doomed from the start.

Four magic words, adequately executed, are the life's blood for any true friendship. Those words are "I'll never say quit." They can be debated, taken apart philosophically, semantically, and rationally, but the truth remains: many times relationships endure and grow because they have to. They are forced to it. They are given no options.

Our culture of convenience denounces that idea as heresy. In a society where instant pain-relief, immediate gratification, and self-expression are a trinity, tenaciousness in relationship is sacrilege.

Perhaps no other biblical story captures the essence of tenacity like the Luke 15 account popularly called "The Story of the Prodigal Son." It is, in reality, "The Story of the Waiting Father." This narrative paints a picture of tenacious love. The father has worked hard all of his life, and his youngest son violates everything from his Jewish culture to common courtesy in asking for his portion of the family inheritance while his father is still living. He proceeds to profane his faith, his family name, and his own integrity before he comes to the end of himself.

When he does, the son heads back to the place where he is known and loved—his father's house. And then we read one of the most poignant passages in the Book: "But while he was still a long way off, his father saw him and was filled with compassion for him; he ran to his son, threw his arms around him and kissed him" (Luke 15:20). The moment that dad had dreamed of had come. Neither his own age nor his son's prior actions would deny him. This was no rush to judgment, but a rush to celebrate. Not a run down a country lane, but a victory lap. Tenacious love had won.

Actually the son had come home for provision, but the old man raced to give him protection. The villagers, who had been angered by his action against his family, actions which had tacitly shamed the community, possibly would have killed him had his father not reached him first.

How many days late into the evening had that father sat outside his door, looking down the road and seeking the familiar motion of his walking son, outlined against the horizon? How many nights had he prayed to Yahweh to keep his son from harm? How many servants had he sent to distant places, seeking word of his boy? And suddenly, there he was!

Leaving his dignity in the doorway of that Palestinian home, the father—no doubt a respected elder in the village—felt the surge of power in aging legs and ancient feet, as he began to walk toward that trudging figure, then a faster walk, then a hobbling run with shouts of joy filling the air: "My son, my son, you're home at last!"

The effusive joy trapped in long nights of longing, prayer, and hope gushed out of him as he lunged into his son with sobs and kisses. Tenacity had won. The self-pitying person, the offendable one, and the easily embarrassed would have given up long before, but the one who loves no matter what stays and gets the joy.

Covenant of Truth-telling

In the Acts 2 passage previously cited, one thing stands out as part of a pattern of developing cohesion between people: they met together daily.

By spending time together, they obviously talked about normal things—work, kids, the future, the excitement of those days in Jerusalem. They were normal folk. It doesn't stretch things too far, I think, to suggest that they shared thoughts and feelings about themselves and their burgeoning relationship with Jesus. They were, in fact, telling the truth about themselves.

As a point of focus, however, they heard the apostles teach about Jesus. These are the men who had been close to Him. They were telling new followers about His ways and His works, just reporting the truth about what He did and the things He said.

These folks were brought together around truth, which is the mortar that holds relationships together. First, I tell myself the truth, then I can tell you the truth.

The New Testament provides a provocative model for the way truth works in a relationship. It is framed in the idea of submission.

Unfortunately, the meaning of *submission* has been often adulterated by our culture and manipulated by self-centered leaders to support their own ends. The very hearing of the word triggers a negative response. Some people react in fear. Some react in anger. In reality the voluntary act of one person submitting to another embodies the most freeing, empowering theme of the New Testament. It begins with truth-telling.

She sat across from me, pale and tense. As gently as I could, I asked whether she would consider her relationship with her husband to be pretty solid. Literally through clenched teeth, she said: "Oh, yes, I'm submitted." Clearly she had some kind of order or system in mind. That idea is found in a variety of places in the New Testament.

But my knee-jerk reflex was, "Lady, you're not submitted. You're a slave!" Whatever *submission* might be, it was not what she was expressing that day.

As an action, submission literally means "to send under or to arrange under." Since it is used most often with personal pronouns, it carries the thrust of sending oneself under (for example, "submit to one another out of reverence for Christ" [Eph. 5:21], and "Humble yourselves, therefore, under God's mighty hand, that He may lift you up in due time" [1 Peter 5:6]).

The context determines the particular slant of the verb usage. The idea of voluntary and mutual submission is very strong in the passage from Ephesians. One gets the sense that it enhances, rather than diminishes, the participants. On the surface, the imperative "submit yourselves to each other" may appear to be burdensome when in truth it really refers to a way in which individuals can be free to feed the relationship.

The critical point is to understand that submission is an act of the will. It is a matter of your choice. You can be forced into slavery, but no one can ever make you submit.

A number of years ago, several young men from the Irish Republican Army died in Maze Prison in Northern Ireland. They starved themselves to death. In that most dramatic way, they were saying to the British government,

"You can flog us, incarcerate us for life, or shoot us, but you can never make us submit."

Submission is just the opposite of subjugation by another. And mutual submission seems to be a warmhearted competition to see who can outgive the other. So when two people choose to submit to each other, they are willingly empowering the relationship with all of their gifts, capabilities, flaws, and dreams. Part of the submission process is captured in disclosing to the other party thoughts, feelings, and knowledge on any given subject or situation. Submission is me telling you the truth about what I think, feel, and know, and trusting you to handle that risk and insight appropriately with great care.

At a conference some time ago, I asked the question, "What do you think of when I say the word 'submissive'?"

One man said, "Passive."

Another said, "A wimp."

A lady commented, "Doormat."

Someone else chimed in, "Mr. Milquetoast."

Then I asked, "Who is the most submissive person in the New Testament?"

And they replied, "Jesus."

"Do any of the definitions you just gave me apply to Him?"

Instantaneously they chorused, "No!"

I said, "Then our *cultural* understanding of submission must be distorted as it relates to the *biblical* understanding of submission."

Here is Jesus, at one and the same time, the most authoritative person and the most submitted person in the New Testament. Two implications arise from that recognition: One is that there is some intimate connection between authority and submission, and the other would be that whatever submission is, it is far from passive!

Looking at submission first, a biblical understanding would suggest taking control of my life under God. Self-control is emulated from the Gospels through the Epistles as a mark of the kingdom and a prerequisite for leadership.

The Gospel record offers a fascinating snapshot of just this point. In the Sermon on the Mount, Jesus said, "If someone strikes you on one cheek, turn to him the other also. If someone takes your cloak, do not stop him from taking your tunic" (Luke 6:29). What a fascinating statement! But it's much more than that. Jesus is speaking out a kingdom truth that permeates His life and death. In today's jargon, He is simply saying, "Everybody and his brother has an agenda and oftentimes they will try to impose that agenda on you. Don't let that happen. I have given you a prior directive, and I will empower you to act on it."

To put it another way, when someone slaps you on the cheek and wants you to return it in kind, he is inviting you to his playing field. When you refuse that invitation by inviting him to your playing field, the entire game changes.

Someone looks at you and says, "You're an idiot!"

Your natural reaction would be to retort, "And your mother wears combat boots!"

Inside he says, "Gotcha!"

But if he says, "You're an idiot!" and you reply, "Are you just finding that out? My friends and family have known that for years," he has nowhere to go. The agenda is no longer his. You have taken his momentum and defused the issue.

In a friendly relationship, self-control is just as important. When I tell the truth by articulating to my friend what I think, feel, and know, I am helping to define our common agenda and choosing to submit myself to the other person. If I remain silent, the agenda will be his or hers by abdication. Poetically silence may be golden, but relationally it's a black hole. I don't know what silence means. It offers no sense of direction and no insight into conflict resolution.

I asked a college president colleague of mine what constituted good administration. He simply said, "Keep on talking. Don't let communication stop until a quality resolution has been produced." That is true for Arab-Israeli negotiations, United Nations conferencing with Serbs and Bosnians, or one-on-one relationships.

Jesus exemplified submission through truth-telling in the final hours of His earthly life. In Gethsemane, needing His friends to be with Him and knowing a terrible end was near, He agonized in His father's presence. He said, "Father, if You are willing, take this cup from Me; yet not My will, but Yours be done" (Luke 22:42). He was simply telling the Father this truth: "Let Me tell You how I feel; if there's any way to avoid the cross, let Me do it. Nevertheless, I trust You." Submission, pure and simple.

A good friend describes it this way: "We take Jesus, and we throw Him on the cross because we can't stand His rightness, saying, 'Take that!' "

Pinioned between heaven and earth by His love and our sin, He said, "Fine, if that's the way it is, that's the way I'll love you. Father, forgive them, because they don't understand." He took the worst thing we could do to Him, turned it around, and redeemed us with it. Submission, powerful and elegant.

When we are called to submission, we are called to self-control. We are called to be in charge of our lives in a way we never have. We are called to an agenda that supersedes natural reactions. Rather than giving up our wills, we submit our wills to God for His empowering in our day-to-day circumstances. In so doing, we bring power and meaning to every relationship we have.

If I truly am a person submitted to God and submitted to the leadership in my company, I will not talk to other employees about seemingly insensitive administrative decisions, but I will speak to my superiors about such matters. In some settings, that is not without risk, but it is full of integrity and full of promise for a quality future.

If I'm submitted to my mate, I will consistently communicate what I think, feel, and know for the sake of the relationship. The same is true of friendship. The same holds true for parent-child discussions.

Prior to the submission of Gethsemane, at the upper-room dinner Jesus had expressed His authority by not exploding in anger at His disciples' jockeying for authority and position in their table talk. Rather, He simply said, if I may paraphrase it, "Let Me show you how real authority expresses itself." And He took a bowl and towel, knelt down, and began to wash their feet.

The kingdom of God really is a disconcerting place because my Western culture tells me that authority stands up and speaks out while submission kneels down and washes feet. Then a carpenter out of Nazareth came along and said, "My kingdom is very different from that. In My kingdom, submission stands up and speaks out and authority kneels down and washes feet." In a biblical relationship, the question is not "Who is in control of this relationship?" but rather "How is this relationship nurtured?" The answer is "I am in control of myself, and I bring that confidence and strength to what we share together."

Thus covenant through submission sets the pace. Time, tenacity, and truth-telling are the tools with which covenant builds the house of friendship. If I know you will give me your time, and I know you're not going to run away when I tell you the truth about what I think, feel, and know, then I can afford to tell you the truth. When that happens, it's the Waiting Father with hugs, kisses, joyous shouts, and a festive table one more time!

*FRIEND is a title earned by
days of being close,
hearing more than words,
sharing each day's hopes,
walking through the fears,
trusting with your heart,
and, in spite of disappointment,
believing for the best.
FRIEND is a title you have earned.*

—**Ruth Foth**

> *"In My father's house are many rooms; if it were not so, I would have told you. I am going there to prepare a place for you."*
>
> *John 14:2*

Chapter 8

The Direction I Face: Dreaming

Tadpoles needed to be very careful around us.

Death and taxes are the certainties of life for adults. But for nine-year-old boys living near a spring-fed lake, it's catching tadpoles.

During my fourth-grade year soon after leaving India, John David and I spent most of our time together—fishing, hiking, sledding, biking, exploring, snowball fights, BB gun wars, self-help ukulele lessons, and . . . tadpole hunts.

Our dads were colleagues at the college just up the road, and we lived only a block from each other. His dad, a leader in the college community, was known for his vision, wisdom, and authentic piety. John's mom was the daughter of a Norwegian sea captain. She was a caring, insightful, gracious lady, who had a gift for gently getting straight to the point. Her kitchen was one of the bases for our forays because it was a good supply center for milk, cookies, and the like.

It was one of those tadpole-safari days. Our purpose

was clear: Catch the biggest tadpoles we could, take them home, and grow them to froghood in our mothers' washtubs in the basement. It was fun. It was biology. It was spring. And somewhere in the mix, we began to dream. Dreaming with John David was terrific because any idea was fair game. He was high energy, intense, inquisitive, bold, always on the run. We decided that he would be a dentist and I would be a mechanical engineer. We would sing in a quartet and travel together. Life would be grand.

The next year, however, I moved from Missouri to California. We stayed in touch off and on over the next thirty years. He graduated from high school in Springfield, Missouri; I graduated from high school in Oakland, California. He went to Yale in New Haven; I went to UC in Berkeley. He graduated from Yale in history; I transferred and graduated from Bethany College of California in theology. He went to the University of Chicago for law school; I went to Wheaton College Graduate School and studied religious education. He became an attorney and taught classes at Southwest Missouri State University in Springfield, Missouri; I became a minister and pioneered a congregation next to the University of Illinois in Urbana. He became auditor and then attorney general for the state of Missouri; I stayed in Urbana for eleven years and then took the presidency of my alma mater, Bethany College. Six years later, my friend John David Ashcroft was elected Republican governor of the state of Missouri, and four years after that was reelected with the largest majority of any governor since the Civil War.

Boyhood dreams may take other forms in adulthood, but they are the stuff of spring days and summer nights. They are the heady delights of young minds and are delicious when shared with a friend. It matters less that they come true than simply that they are. And for a dream to be shared with another is to root it deep in that person as well, for my dream is called to account by your awareness.

History-giving is the basis for relationship, affirmation nurtures it, and covenant makes it secure. But dream-sharing is the fuel that makes that friendship fly!

Dreams and hopes go together. To hope is to have meaning, no matter how farfetched or fanciful it might appear at first glance. Hope, after all, is part of the trilogy—faith, hope, and love—that endures forever.

Jesus was a dreamer. His teachings in the last few weeks of His earthly life were succinct, powerful, and directional. John's Gospel commits almost half of its content to those days and those teachings. The setting was the Last Supper. Judas had just left to trigger the event that would become the watershed of human history. Jesus made some comments about being glorified—His work coming to completion. Then He riveted the disciples with this statement:

> [Jesus said,] "A new command I give you: Love one another. As I have loved you, so you must love one another. By this all men will know that you are My disciples, if you love one another."
> Simon Peter asked Him, "Lord, where are You going?"
> Jesus replied, "Where I am going, you cannot follow now, but you will follow later."
> Peter asked, "Lord, why can't I follow You now? I will lay down my life for You."
> Then Jesus answered, "Will you really lay down your life for Me? I tell you the truth, before the rooster crows, you will disown Me three times!" (John 13:34-38)

The words hang in the air like breath on a subzero morning. Simon the Less and Andrew shift positions uncomfortably, glancing down.

Jesus and the burly disciple's eyes lock in understanding. It's the gentle, matter-of-fact quality in Jesus' voice that holds Peter. As the momentary zeal flashing in his own eyes starts to fade, the Master's eyes hold him. As it were, the earth opens under his feet, but he is transfixed by those eyes.

The voice speaks again filling the abyss beneath Peter,

"But, don't worry, I'm going to My Father's house to prepare a place for you. I'll be back to get you."

Simon the Less and Andrew swivel their heads in one motion to look at the two. Peter almost imperceptibly relaxes his diaphragm and slowly lets his breath out. The tightness in his forearms and clenched hands releases and finds its way to his throat. And it's all right. The time for words is past. The one who boasts he will die for his friend is gently overwhelmed by the One who will do exactly that before another day has passed without a boast or backward glance.

How could this brawny man, feeling like a little boy, know that in just a matter of weeks everything would change? How could he know that he, the wave-man, would become the rock-man? How could he know that his boasts would be transformed into Life-giving phrases at the Feast of Pentecost? How could he know that 3,000 people would burst into the kingdom at the hearing of his words?

He couldn't. He couldn't dream it. But Someone could. And did.

It is precisely because they had spent time, shared history, and walked through deep waters together that Jesus could dream out loud for His friend and follower. There is a sense in which Jesus' dream for Peter proclaims a place of security and serenity for anyone who will listen. For sure, it becomes the prototype for human relationships because, and I say it again, they are based in history, nurtured by affirmation and commitment, but driven by dreams.

We don't speak here of nighttime dreams—those millisecond flashes of imagery that are remembered only fleetingly or not at all. We speak of those daytime dreams that swell and elongate from deep within our spirits as we contemplate what might be.

Some years ago, I was asked what has now become something of a common question: "If you could do anything in the world and you knew you could not fail, what would you do?" That simple question has stayed with me for twenty years. In fact, it has given rise to some reflection that probably would never have happened had I not been challenged in that way. Dreams are essential to a meaningful existence. Life without dreams is no life at all.

One of the most frightening things about the gang activities erupting in major cities across the United States is found in the interviews conducted by news reporters with gang members. When asked why the killing is occurring, the response is usually some territorial reason, such as "They're on our turf." But when asked if he or she is afraid of dying, the response is often sullen and succinct: "What is there to live *for?*" Without hope, without a dream, life loses not only quality but also ultimate meaning. The vicious, viral contagion spawned by that hopelessness is threatening American society in a way that few things have in this century.

Flying out of Johannesburg, South Africa in apartheid days, I struck up a conversation with my seatmate, a young Pakistani businessman. When I inquired about his business, he told me he was in electronics. When I asked about his history, he said that he had been raised in South Africa, but that he no longer lived there. I asked him why, and he said, "I tried to get an office in the city so I could conduct my business, but because of my race, my color, I was not allowed to do so. So after a number of years of trying, I moved to Dallas, Texas and have become very successful in the electronics industry."

Naively, I asked, "What's the toughest thing about the policy of apartheid?"

Without batting an eye, he looked at me with great seriousness and said, "It takes away hope . . . it takes away hope."

Several years later, Delta Flight 40 pulled up sharply over the International Airport at Bucharest, Romania, as the pilot said, "A light is indicating a possible malfunction of the landing gear, and we need to go around again. We think everything's OK, but want to make sure." In a few minutes we touched down without incident. And thus began a five-day adventure in that land locked between Russia, Bulgaria, Yugoslavia, and the Black Sea. The land of abundant, real natural resources and the unreal supernatural Count Dracula. A land that had been raped by Hitler and was held under the tyrannical thumb of Nicolae Ceausescu until December of 1989 when a Christmas miracle happened. Between followers of Jesus, university students, mild weather, and a disgruntled army, the four-decade reign of the communist dictator Ceausescu came tumbling down.

We had come to Romania at the invitation of Assist International's President Bob Pagett. A friend of many years, Bob had urged several of us to go with him to meet with the leadership of the country to determine how we could better use U.S. resources—dollars, material, and people—to continue Romania's march toward democracy and religious freedom. Bob and Charlene Pagett had invested much of themselves in the previous four years to befriend and help the Romanian people.

The country had attempted its own share of landings in the arena of democracy and continued to grapple with conditions and groups that potentially worked against a safe landing. Our purpose was to assist and support the followers of Jesus in that society as they did their part to ensure free and democratic institutions in accordance with their function as leaven in Romanian society.

A team of eight went. The point man with the government was then Governor John Ashcroft. The days were compressed with meetings that were exceptionally instructive. What we found was this: just beneath the surface of the relatively newfound freedoms were many people who nursed an incipient fear that this phase of Romanian history could also change overnight. Their fear was not some vague, unspecified anxiety. The fear was very specific. They were fundamentally afraid to hope, and that fear was paralyzing. It gives rise to speech-making, but does not precipitate action.

Hope is the tensile strength of a dream. Tomorrow is another day. The sun will come up. I'll have another opportunity. I can go on from there.

We can hear it in the language people use. There have been numbers of speeches made in this century that are burned into our national psyches in such a way that we conjure them up instantaneously in the right setting. For some it is Franklin Roosevelt saying, "The only thing we have to fear is fear itself." For others it is Douglas MacArthur leaving the Philippines, proclaiming, "I shall return." To another it is the aging, tenacious Winston Churchill intoning, "We shall fight them on the beaches and in the fields." For another it might be John F. Kennedy, saying at the Berlin Wall, "Ich bin ein Berliner." There is an entire generation from the 1960s, however, who will never forget Martin Luther King, Jr., crying, "I have a dream." That line strikes at the core of all who are essentially human.

We all have dreams—things that if others knew, they might laugh, challenge, or even deride. But real dreams die hard. They are made of resurrection stuff. Bludgeoned by people or circumstances, they just come back brighter, larger, and more intensely.

I have a friend, Dallas Holm. We shared speaking responsibilities some years ago at a ski retreat in Colorado. He told a story of being in a college class where the question was asked, "What do you want to be doing ten years from now?" The reponses were uniform, predictable, and the *religiously correct* answers for that setting.

On the other hand, he said, "I want to have my own Gospel band, travel, and record. I want to write my own songs!" The response could have been no more cool than if he had an eye in the middle of his forehead! At the time he articulated that dream, almost thirty years ago, no music group like that really existed. But in the next twenty years, he became a leader among myriads of Gospel singers around the world. He lived out his dream.

Upon arriving as president of Bethany College, I met a young man from Puerto Rico. I'll call him Roberto. Roberto had landed in California from San Juan two years before with no money and little English. He had not followed the required application procedure. He had not taken the TOEFL exam, the English proficiency test required of most international students. He had nothing except the prayers of his parents and a dream.

A fellow classmate named Tim, a North American raised in Argentina, befriended him. He and Roberto agreed on the dream. Tim would translate recordings Roberto made of his classes. He helped the young Puerto Rican learn English phrases to use in social situations. Roberto began to excel.

At the conclusion of my second year as president of the college, during the graduation ceremonies, he walked with confidence to the podium as the student commencement speaker! In his opening remarks, he thanked Tim for his friendship and commitment. Then, turning to his parents in the grandstands on his left, he said in Spanish, "Mom and Dad, this is for you!" and proceeded to deliver one of the most stirring addresses I've ever heard at a college commencement, in perfect English.

Another story to illustrate the power of a dream comes to mind. I have a friend whom I met in Bangalore, South India in 1973. She was in her seventies. Anna Tomaseck was quite a lady. In 1924, she broke her engagement to a fine young medical student in Ohio because she had a dream he couldn't share. She dreamed of going to India to give her life to the poorest of the poor, not in Calcutta like Mother Teresa, but in the northernmost reaches of the country. She served in that place for fifty-two years, and with coworkers over those years she raised 400 orphans to adulthood.

One night in Bangalore, a speaker finished his remarks,

saying, "Anna Tomaseck, if you'd give fifty-two years to Jesus and India again, I want you to come down here to the front." I watched as she made her way painfully out of her seat, three rows from the back of the auditorium, and started down the aisle. Painfully, I say, because she wore slippers over swollen feet. She was no stranger to pain — tuberculosis as a girl, and seven surgeries for cancer as an adult. But this time it was different. Two weeks before in a Calcutta hospital, she had been found to have filaria — elephantitus — in her legs. It hardly slowed her down.

I will not soon forget her face or her words as she shuffled past us down the aisle. With head thrown back and tears streaming down her cheeks, I heard her say over and over, "I'd do it a million times. I'd do it a million times. I'd do it a million times!"

When Anna later came to our college to speak, she took the students by storm with her vision and her stories. We would sit on the chapel platform, Anna and I, to talk about love and leadership and power . . . long before this book entered my imagination. She would regale us with stories humorous, heartrending, and triumphant. When I asked her for a favorite, she told this one.

"Early one morning in the village of Rupadiah, way up in sugarcane country on the border of Nepal, my coworker and I heard a knock at the door. We opened it to find an Indian man standing there with a cloth-wrapped bundle in his arms. When the bundle began to move, he quickly explained what had happened.

"In our village there was no sewer system, only a dung heap outside of town where the villagers went to relieve themselves. He had gone out there early in the morning, and something moving under a pile of leaves at the base of a tree caught his eye. He brushed away the leaves and looked at the face of a newborn baby girl, umbilical cord and placenta still attached, and quite disgruntled with her predicament!

"Apparently some Indian gypsies had come through

during the night and dumped the infant by the dung heap. Baby girls in that day, and with those people, were disposable.

"He had brought her to us because he knew we would care for her. He was right. My coworker and I, however, were caring for twenty-three children at the time, and nine of them were nursing infants. We didn't get much sleep, but our prayer life was incredible!

"We kept her until she was seven, at which time she was adopted by a wealthy family in New Delhi. Over the years, we corresponded intermittently.

"Twenty years passed, and one day we received a letter from London, England with a photograph inside. Then we understood the in-between pieces.

"After a little while in her home in New Delhi, her adoptive parents had discovered she had an ear for music. They gave her piano lessons, and she took to it with amazing speed. She became so proficient that at age sixteen they sent her to the London Conservatory of Music. She went on to become a concert pianist.

"The photo in the letter was a picture of her with Princess Margaret at Buckingham Palace following a concert for the royal family."

It's a long way from a dung heap on the border of Nepal to Buckingham Palace. And it's a long way from a dream in Ohio to a reality in North India. But a dream takes more than the dreamer with it. People who never had an inkling or a chance get caught in its current, and they get swept along to magnificent places they never imagined they could be. I think of that fact, now and again, when I happen to hear a sonata or an etude on the piano.

But how does the sharing of a dream build relationship? It's simply this: If I can trust you to love me in my past (history-giving), and if I can trust you to love me in my present (affirmation, confrontation, commitment), maybe, just maybe, I can trust you to love me in my tomorrow.

When another dreams with and for me, my dream

moves to a different level—a mom and dad who believe I can do it; a partner who does extra duty so I'm free to pursue a vision; a friend who won't leave it alone.

Something marvelous happens when I share a dream with a friend. When I articulate the shape of what I see, the real me stands up. I not only am, but I am becoming. In my adult life, I am probably never so much a child as when I speak out my dreams. Innocent, virginal, unsullied. My history is not so; my present is not so, only my future is so.

The Apostle Paul captured that idea again in the first chapter of Philippians.

And this is my prayer: that your love may abound more and more in knowledge and depth of insight, so that you may be able to discern what is best and may be pure and blameless until the day of Christ, filled with the fruit of righteousness that comes through Jesus Christ—to the glory and praise of God (Phil. 1:9-11).

His dream for the Philippians was that a kind of clearseeing would prevail. He did not wish them things or circumstances, but rather perception and insight. In fact, he suggested that if that dream came true, they would be full of the fruit of righteousness. The kind of encouragement that comes through articulated dreams for each other moves us toward their realization. We not only need to dream dreams for ourselves and share them with each other, but we also need to learn to dream dreams for our friends.

Some years ago I participated in a funeral in Wheaton, Illinois. The other minister gave the message and this insightful illustration: "When I was growing up, my dad allowed me to play baseball, but he never came to any of my ball games. He was conservative in the extreme, always wearing a dark-blue suit and a tie. I think he may have slept in a tie.

"In the spring of my senior year, our team had played well and made it to the championship game. I went to my father and begged him to come to the game, but he wouldn't commit himself.

"On that May afternoon, I walked out onto the ball field, looked up into the stands, and saw a sea of brightly attired baseball fans. And there, right in the middle of them, in his blue suit, was my father. I was thrilled.

"We played our hearts out, but by the time we got to the bottom of the ninth inning, we were still down by three runs. The score was four to one; there were two outs; the bases were loaded; and it was my turn to bat.

"I walked to the plate, knocked the dirt out of my cleats with my bat, assumed my batting stance, and the pitcher put one right down the middle. I swung. Strike one.

"I backed out of the box, banged my cleats again, and got ready. Another fastball. Strike two.

"And then three balls. It was a full count. The crowd was going wild. As I stepped to the plate for my final attempt, I said: 'God, if You are there, *this* is the time!' The ball was pitched, I swung and connected, driving the ball deep to center field. I took off for first, and as I rounded first, the first man scored. As I raced into second, the second man scored. The ball had come off the center field fence, and the center fielder was about to grab it for the throw to the plate.

"Coming around second, I was running as hard as I could. The crowd was on their feet, screaming at the top of their lungs, when all of a sudden above everyone else . . . above all the other voices, I heard my dad. He was shouting, 'IT'S OK, SON, YOU'RE GONNA MAKE IT, COME ON HOME!' I streaked around third, slid in under the tag, and we won the game. And I didn't care. All I could think of was my dad. In my mind's eye for the rest of my life I would see my father on his feet, shouting me home!"

When someone dreams with me and for me, it shifts affirmation into the passing gear. It adds a profound dimension to any relationship because it drives a stake into the future and pulls us toward it.

And that's how the kingdom really is. A God who dreams great dreams for us. A God who adds on special rooms to His home for each one of us. Throws a party, sends out invitations, and stands on the balcony of the heavens, shouting across the galaxies: "IT'S OK, CHILDREN, I'LL HELP YOU MAKE IT, COME ON HOME!"

In the same way, when you round the bases of relationship-building—shared history, mutual affirmation, specific covenants, and shared dreams—there's reason for shouting. For you have closed the circle on themes that will become part of your very fabric, if you work at it daily.

But there's one more facet of relationship that is worthy of your attention. It is the mystery in you, which we will call spirit.

WHEN THE GIANT LIES DOWN

A Dream...

Just a thought...
some grand little scheme,
tucked into a corner,
too shy to reappear.
And you knew it!
Nudged it out of me
into reality.

And you ask
why I love you?!

—Ruth Foth

> *"Deep calls to deep."*
>
> *Psalm 42:7*

Chapter 9

The Connection I Know: Spirit

Spirit is deep—deeper than the cortex of the brain. Beyond history, affirmation, covenant, and dreaming is spirit. To borrow Robert Munger's metaphor of years past, I see my life as a home. When the walls come down little by little, I let you wander into the rooms of my life. You settle in the overstuffed chair by the fire and begin thumbing through old family scrapbooks. As you do that, you get closer to my spirit.

When you walk into the kitchen and sense my appetites or browse in the library of my mind, sensing my thoughts and imaginations, you get closer to my spirit.

If you sit in the worn cane rocker on the porch and look across the fields toward the distant sea on an autumn afternoon, you can sense my past and my future—mellow and crisp, stable yet moving, at one and the same time. You're getting closer to my spirit.

Spirit is the part of my person that connects me with God, who Himself is Spirit. My body may house my spirit, but it cannot restrict or contain it. I can go beyond.

I learned something about spirit one day in November standing in a hospital doorway. A therapist was working with my friend, Dennis, trying to bring him back from the shadow world caused by brain damage.

It had been almost six months since the March Friday morning when he had fallen out of his chair in his Daniel Street home in Champaign, Illinois.

Arrhythmic heart failure triggered the convulsions that racked his body. The doctor's comment was, "Cardiac arrest at age twenty-eight." We were to have met that day for lunch to determine whether or not Dennis would be leaving his position at East Central Illinois Campus Life, where he was the associate director. We had asked him to join the staff of our church as campus pastor at the University of Illinois.

We never had lunch. Instead, I raced to the hospital at 10:30 A.M., responding to a frantic phone call from Ruth, who alerted me that something terrible had happened to Denny. I reached Burnham Hospital just in time to see the doctors place the electrical shock paddles on his chest. In the course of the next hour, his heart started and then stopped beating at least five times.

In response to my questions, the neurologist explained that the heart operates on electrical impulse rhythmically day in and day out. If for some reason those impulses are short-circuited, that three-quarter-pound pump, which regulates life for seventy years, goes into fibrillation. In layperson's terms, it starts quivering like a bowl of jelly. When that happens, the pumping action ceases, and the first place to lose quantities of blood and oxygen is the cortical structure of the brain. The cerebral cortex is the inch-thick covering of the brain, which houses everything from motor responses to memory, critical thinking to comprehension. It literally is the human nerve center, and when it's robbed of oxygen, it's robbed of life.

In an older person those nonregenerative cortical brain

cells can begin to die in two to three minutes. In a younger person it can be four to five minutes. A human has been known to exist for thirty days or more without food and up to three days without water. A few minutes without oxygen, however, ends it all.

Denny was blue by the time the paramedics got him to Burnham Hospital trauma unit. It took them well over an hour to establish even a ragged rhythm in his heart. The doctors' prognosis was "a 10 percent chance to live through the night, and at best a vegetable existence after that."

Those of us who really knew and loved him prayed earnestly for physical and emotional healing. We tried to follow every biblical injunction concerning healing we could find, but nothing happened. My frustration with his condition bordered on rage. I would go daily to Room 243, lay hands on him, and pray. From my hurting disadvantage point, God was deaf.

That rage boiled over one day as I stood by Denny's bed. He was just there. Noncommunicative. Incontinent. Strapped down. Grunting and growling like some primeval thing. Denny might be somewhere in that restless frame, but I sure couldn't find him. I growled too: "God, I believe the spirit of man lives in the cortex of the human brain and when the cortex is damaged, that person is no longer human."

I could almost hear God's response: "Oh, great. Foth, again!" In spite of my feeble attempts to explain Denny's condition, God was gracious. All He had to do was exhale and blow me off the planet. But He didn't.

Leaving Denny's room, I walked into the elevator. Finding myself alone, I slammed my fist into the elevator wall. Hand throbbing, I spit out the classic question through clenched teeth: "Why? What's the sense in all this? He's got a wife and two little girls . . . a significant heart for young people. Why?"

When we are in intense pain, some questions we ask

God are unanswerable. C.S. Lewis certainly came to that conclusion in his book *A Grief Observed:*

Can a mortal ask questions which God finds unanswerable? Quite easily, I should think. All nonsense questions are unanswerable. How many hours are there in a mile? Is yellow square or round? Probably half the questions we ask—half our great theological and metaphysical problems—are like that (© 1961 by N.W. Clerk and HarperCollins Publishers).

On the other hand, there are questions that are authentic and that God certainly can answer, but our frame of reference is too small to comprehend. If a small child comes to me and asks, "What is nuclear physics?" I would try to explain that phenomenon in terms of the atom, using such concrete objects as an apple and an orange. I would indicate that the apple is the center of the atom, and even though you can't really see this atom, it has smaller things inside of it called protons and neutrons. "This orange," I would say, "is one of many other little things that go 'round and 'round this center part. And these atoms are so small that you can't see one by itself. But your body is made up of billions of these." The little kid would look at himself or herself in the mirror and say, "Oh, wow, I've got billions of apples and oranges all over my body." My explanation was essentially correct, but the child's frame of reference was not large enough to comprehend it.

When that happens in human tragedies and we ask God, "Why?" He can explain it. We just can't get our minds around it.

The most debilitating part of my odyssey with Denny was the sense of personal loss. Like having a friend lost at night in a cave, I kept calling into the labyrinthine darkness, hoping for a response. But the only sound I could hear was my own echo, discordant and far away—an off-pitch wind chime in a gusting breeze. Then nothing.

He had to be in there somewhere, lost in that inert trap

of bone and tissue. "Speak to me, Denny. I can hear you breathing. You can come out now. We want you back. If I talk loud enough and long enough, you'll find your way out again."

Then came that April day when I pulled into our driveway on Shurts Street in Urbana and Ruth came running out of the house toward the car. As I rolled down the window, she shouted, "The hospital called, and Denny spoke."

I threw the car into reverse and raced to Burnham Hospital. Running up to the second floor nurses' station, I choked out the question, "Is it true that Denny McNabb spoke?"

The nurse replied, "Yes, sir."

I asked, "Are you sure? It would be a horrible delusion for the family if you aren't sure."

"Yes," she explained, "we always talk to someone in a comatose state. This morning when we took the food tube out, we asked Denny, 'Do you want more orange juice now?' And he said, 'Later.' "

He had started his journey back! As hope was reborn in every fiber of me, I burst into his room and started talking to him. But my articulate, urbane, witty friend still lay there in restraints, tied simultaneously to fleshly existence and what I felt to be subhuman life by 1/8 inch I.V.s. I talked to him, and he didn't respond. His eyes just rolled around in his head like some wounded animal. The person who had once been my friend, my coworker, was an amorphous something without rhyme, reason, or future—trapped in a 230-pound body.

Finally, after what seemed like an hour of futile prodding and talking, I walked to the heavy hospital door, closed it, then went over and grabbed him by the shoulders, lifted him partially off the bed, shook him, and shouted, "Denny, can you hear me?"

Without focusing his eyes, he took a deep breath and said, "Yep."

I went crazy! I just knew that everything was going to be all right. I'd walk in the next day, and he would be sitting up, asking for food.

Wrong again. I entered his room the next day to find him just the way he had been for the last month. But slowly, very slowly over the next several months, Denny started to return. Physically he got stronger. Though disoriented and very shaky, he began to walk. And then against all medical odds, he began to speak. At first, just a few words, then more words, and then disjointed phrases. The medical community calls it aphasia—that condition characterized by sentences constructed appropriately in the brain, but garbled by the time they are spoken, single words or phrases jumbled like pick-up sticks.

In the midst of all the apparent progress, the single most vital component was nowhere to be found: his memory. It had been six months since the heart attack. Denny was sitting up and talking now, but he had lost his history. Short-term memory was shot. Long-term memory was sporadic.

The ability to choose, rationally and volitionally, makes one human. So does the ability to recall and articulate experience through this marvelous device called memory. Loss of memory slaps humanity in the face. Ask anybody who lives with an Alzheimer's victim or a senile grandma.

Members of the medical and therapeutic community who work with brain-damaged persons make it abundantly clear that what we don't know about memory far outdistances what we do know. But two things are certain: Memory is the repository of information, impressions, and feelings that uniquely shape our view of the world and create personality. It is also the link to any relationships we have.

When the cortical structure of the brain suffers violent damage, the memory bank is robbed. If I'm part of your memory bank, and if the bank is robbed, I'm gone. Our relationship no longer exists. More than that, the person who has been traumatized changes.

Denny had the mentality of an infant. He didn't know his extremities were connected to his body. If someone gave him an object, he'd automatically put it in his mouth, just like a baby.

He didn't know anyone—his wife, kids, friends. He vaguely thought he was in Zion, Illinois, his boyhood home. Short-term memory loss made conversation a virtual impossibility. I'd go to see him, and he'd say, "Hi! What's your name?"

I'd respond, "Dick."

He'd say, "Oh, well, what's your name?"

I'd say, "Dick."

He'd respond, "Have I asked you your name?"

That incessant, frustrating redundancy demoralized family and colleagues. It seemed easier to stay away from the body that looked like our loved one, but housed a different person.

On a November morning I walked into that context. Stopping behind the therapist, I listened to her questions as she held up a picture of a cup. "What is this, Denny?" she asked him.

"I don't know."

"It's a cup, Denny."

"What's a cup?"

"You put water into it."

"What's water?"

"You drink it."

"What's drink?"

As I eavesdropped on that one-sided litany of noncomprehension, I suddenly had an idea. Spirit is the deepest part of a human being, lasting forever, as Scripture indicates, and if Scripture lasts forever, perhaps there would be a connection. I turned to Denny, who remembered nothing and no one, and asked: "Denny, do you remember this: 'For God so loved the world, He gave His only begotten Son'?"

After I asked my question, he turned to me, got a far-away look in his eyes, and said, "That if I believe in Him, I won't die anymore!"

The nurse almost passed out. Stunned, I began to cry. I asked, "Denny, do you know this?" I began to sing, "Jesus Loves Me This I Know." He picked it up on key and sang it all the way to the end.

The Spirit of the Lord spoke to me as clearly as I've ever heard anything when He said, "Spirit is deeper than the cortex of the brain."

Today, almost two decades later, Denny has not fully recovered, but enough progress has been made to allow him to function adequately in a residential facility in southern Wisconsin.

In spite of the sadness of Denny's situation, certain vignettes from those days helped us chuckle. Denny's humor was a key part of his personality. With the cortical damage, his wit virtually disappeared until one day some months after his heart attack. He had been a lifeguard in his youth, and I thought swimming might revitalize and stimulate his brain. So we took off for the closest pool.

As we got into the shallow end, he splashed the water and said, "What is this stuff?"

"It's water," I replied.

"Sure does burn your eyes," he retorted.

"Well, that's chlorine."

"What's chlorine?"

"It helps keep disease away."

"What's disease?"

"Forget it, McNabb. Come on down here to the deeper water and swim!"

He queried, "What's swim? How do I do that? Like this?" He began to dog paddle.

"Close enough. Let's go," I said, as I moved deeper.

In moments we were splashing around in eight-foot water, and I thought, "He's coming back!"

Just then, I turned, and he was gone! Underwater. In

rapid fire my mind raced. *Where is he? How'm I gonna get his 230 pounds out of here?*

About that time he bobbed up next to me, spit out a mouthful of water through his grin, and exclaimed, "Boy, you sure can't sit down out here, can you?"

I couldn't help it. I laughed. He did too. It was old times.

Denny's story is not unique. Families down the street and around the world are facing the same challenges, trying to answer unanswerable questions, struggling to cope with overwhelming circumstances, and learning to live out a new definition of trust. Edna Hong, in her book *Turn Over Any Stone*, lets the reader participate in her struggle to find peace in the midst of the pain of dealing with her mentally retarded granddaughter, Nani. She questions:

> *Is being absent-in-mind*
> *synonymous with being absent-in-spirit?*
> *To have faith do we need to have enough mind to grasp*
> *the meaning of faith?*
> *To be in the relationship of faith to God the Father,*
> *do we need a measurable IQ?*

An answer comes to her after lonely hours spent in contemplation and prayer:

> *The meaning of life is in the relationship*
> *of the whole person to God,*
> *Not in the relationship of the cerebellum.*
> *The relationship to God is possible in Christ*
> *for every individual*
> *from Einstein — to Nani.*

In response to the illness of her dear friend's father, a gifted leader, who in old age "simply lay and babbled numbers," Hong writes a powerful eulogy:

> *When the tenuous tape coiled on the reel of his memory*
> *no longer tensible*
> *broke*
> *and in his patching and repairing*
> *he fused incompatible pieces,*

WHEN THE GIANT LIES DOWN

When the tenacious thread of memory
frayed and flaccid
slackened, bunched, knotted
and finally unraveled
into a tortuous, twisted tangle,

When others heard the twang of breaking memory
and saw the shattered fragments of what was mind
and murmured sorrowfully,
"How tragic!
He was a giant in his day!"

The Lord God picked up the fumbled, jumbled words
the topsy-turvey alphabet
the whole embarrassing litter
and it was as if they rearranged themselves
into a liturgy of praise!

And it was so.
The Lord God looked
and, behold, it was very good.

When the contours of ideas blurred and eclipsed
the colors of emotions faded out
and words themselves grew vague and meaningless,
when even word-sounds
vowels and consonants
retained no meaning.

When — strangely —
as he lay in his long dying —
numbers became his living language
and he intoned them one by one
tirelessly
hour upon hour
day after day
as time tallied its final count for him,

When others stood beside his bed
and heard his babbling numbers
and tiptoed tearfully away,

the Lord God gathered up the digits and the ciphers
the sum total of his numbers
the whole untidy chaos
and they added up!
and their sum was — adoration!

And it was so.
The Lord God looked
and, behold, it was very good.
(used by permission of Edna Hong)

As I reflect on Mrs. Hong's poignant and moving insights, it occurs to me that she is saying something profound about human relationships. If I understand it right, when we are unable to communicate with other humans or they with us, the Spirit of God can go deeper.

We are designed for intimacy with God and intimacy with each other. When the mechanism we call the brain breaks off human interaction, apparently the spirit is not inhibited by that breakdown. A memory at a deeper level continues to function.

I cannot prove that scientifically. It is not measurable, but it is observable. I've seen it over and over again. Spirit is like the wind; we only observe and try to understand.

In the spring of 1993, I told part of Denny's story at a seminary near Boston. At the conclusion of the chapel, a young man came directly to me and said, "I've got to tell you something.

"I'm an intern at a church near here, and last week they sent me to see an old lady who had been in a nursing home for a long time. All she did was lay there and babble.

"After I talked to her for some time and received no response at all, I said, 'Mrs. Fredericks, would you like me to pray before I leave?'

"Instantly she was lucid. Turning over, she looked right at me and said, 'I'd like to say something first!'

"I said, 'Fine.' She began to quote Psalm 119. Psalm 119

has 176 verses! I grabbed my Bible and followed along. She quoted it word for word.

"Finishing the psalm, she prayed a beautiful prayer. Saying 'Amen,' she slipped back into her other world!"

In nursing facilities and institutions around the world, one can find thousands of people trapped in damaged minds. They sit in a circle wedged in place by time and circumstance, repositories of prior knowledge, a composite of wisdom past. Homemakers, aeronautical engineers, thoracic surgeons, truckers, and philosophers, strapped in wheelchairs, mute for months on end. A Stonehenge convalescent home.

Then, one day, a visiting pianist sits down at the spinet and starts playing an old anthem. Slowly at first the gentleman in the far corner, eleven years ago a brilliant physicist in a Midwestern university, begins to mouth syllables. Hesitant sound soon follows, as somewhere deep in that seventy-nine-year-old man, synapses fire and a melody sung as a child in his Ohio village church surfaces. Memory is triggered. Nerves stimulate vocal chords. By the second verse, tears and a smile vie for a place on that weathered face as the light of recognition flickers deep in his eyes.

It is easy to speak of people with powerful bodies and towering intellects. We admire them. But what of the person who has neither? A person of weakened body and damaged intellect?

Reaching out to the weakest of the weak—those with no intellectual currency to spend—is what Bethlehem is all about. Bethlehem—that insignificant, faraway place. The unsanitary cave barn with all of its drawbacks is precisely the place where the Giant lay down. It was a place of adoration, promise, and misunderstanding all at the same time.

In a stratified world of class consciousness, caste, and pecking order, God levels the playing field by saying, "The essential part of you is spirit, which is designed to connect with me. Don't forget that."

The difference between a Nobel laureate and a withered person who stares blankly at a pale-green hospital wall is a millisecond—the time it takes for a human skull to smash into the doorpost of a $50,000 Mercedes hit from the side by a truck running a red light. A millisecond can turn the world upside down. We are not gods. We are fragile beyond measure.

One day the obituary in a local newspaper will read: "Foth died on such-and-such a date." Don't you believe it. My body just fell off. My spirit will still be alive.

The biblical story says I'll get a new body, not subject to decay and death. One in which I can go to my Father's house for dinner. Dinner's big with me. Dinner was big with Denny. New cortex and new body. All things will be new forever.

On that day, Denny and Nani and Mrs. Fredericks will be whole—in perfect relationship with God and each other. So will we.

WHEN THE GIANT LIES DOWN

Fragile, restless spirit,
deepest part of me,
how you long to be
connected at the core
to the Creator;
so that I can find . . .
meaning,
identity,
and peace.

—Ruth Foth

Chapter 10

The Move I Make: Risk

The two men moved out tentatively, one leading the other by the hand. The one behind squeezed his eyes shut and tugged back hesitantly on the leader.

One hundred and ninety-eight other men in teams of two began walking in all directions across an expansive grassy area next to the rural highway in south-central Illinois. Passing motorists did double takes!

Presently, the hands were dropped, and verbal instructions ensued from leader to follower. The noise grew as more people chimed in. Volume and range of voices clashed, each jockeying for airspace. Leaders repeated themselves, and followers strained to catch the right voice.

We were on a men's retreat trustwalk, an exercise designed to illustrate trust and encourage unity among the men. At first glance, it appeared to fit in the category of twenty-nine verses of "Kumbayah" around the campfire. In reality, however, this experiment would promote reflection and discussion that persisted through the rest of the retreat.

The idea is straightforward: One person closes his eyes, and his partner leads him anywhere on the grounds, first by holding his hand and then by verbal command. After ten minutes the roles are reversed. Excitement grows as dozens of teams compete for the same walking space, with one person in each team moving blind. The learning curve elevates to about 75 degrees!

Amid laughter and horseplay, the conferees returned to the auditorium, and the question was posed: "At what point did you, as a follower, feel like opening your eyes?"

One man exclaimed, "When I felt the tree! In the sunlight, the shadow of the tree fell across my face, and I knew I was in trouble. I actually opened my eyes and sure enough, there was a tree. But it was fifty feet away over on the left. The late afternoon sun had given the tree a long shadow. It wasn't real, but it certainly felt real!"

Another man said, "I became anxious when instructions were imprecise. Like 'You're coming to some stairs sometime soon.'"

Still another chuckled, "For me it was when directions came too late. Like 'That was a log!'"

Finally, a man in his eighties broke in and said, "I didn't open my eyes at all. That was one of the most exhilarating things I've done in a long time." When asked "Why?" he replied, "Because that's one of the only times in my life when someone else was responsible for the obstacles!"

He had caught one of the primary points of the exercise—trusting the leader's willingness and ability to take the follower adventuring and protect him at the same time. The other point, of course, was to illustrate the challenging, complex nature of leadership. Things like, decisions aren't made in a vacuum; awareness of surroundings is imperative; and directions have to be clearly spoken and reinforced.

I once interviewed a man in his late seventies in front of

600 college students. Since he had been a corporate head for many years, I asked him the standard question about leadership: "What does it take to be a good leader?" Without hesitation he replied, "The ability to articulate vision clearly, to make decisions, and," pausing, with mischief in his eyes, "to anticipate what's coming over the next hill!"

Leadership books are replete with lists of attributes characteristic of leaders. One of the best analyses I've read comes from Howard Haas' recent book *The Leader Within*. Haas is the former president and CEO of Sealy, Incorporated. He says leaders do the following:

> *They use imagination. They are open. They synthesize. They take risks. They take a long-term view. They are interested in initiative. They are active. They are interested in discovery. They seek alternatives. They are interested in content. They are involved with strategy. They are experimental. They are inductive. They are firm. They are dynamic (© 1992 by Howard G. Haas and Bob Tamarkin and HarperCollins Publishers).*

I see those things as really being true, but that old Illinois gentleman's unwitting and spontaneous description of leadership, "one who takes responsibility for the obstacles," intrigues me. Is that leadership or just paternalism? Maybe leadership should be "one who doesn't run away from the obstacles." Or "one who doesn't simply tell you how to do something, but shows you how."

Well, whatever the definition, two things are clear: How leaders invest their time indicates their values, and how leaders deal with people indicates their value to the leaders. A couple of the most painful and embarrassing moments in my fourteen years as a college president came when I didn't invest enough time in thorough research before making a decision. It was not just working through data, but also not talking with the folks whom the decision would impact. Similarly, meaningful time spent with associates in every level of the organization speaks volumes to everyone.

Now those two thoughts from my experience are hardly original. Men and women with far more range and expertise have noted these fundamentals before, and in great depth. I, however, would make this observation: Where the giving of time and compassionate action intersect, the connection between love, leadership, and power manifests itself.

As we lead in the home, the Girl Scout troop, academe, business, the church, and government, we owe it to ourselves and to those for whom we care to grapple with how those three qualities connect. They really do have a common thread, but one has to stand in the right place to see it. As with photography, a little adjustment to the size of the frame or a step to one side or the other can radically change the picture. The essential question here is, "What is the desired relationship between love, leadership, and power?" That query cannot be answered without personalizing it.

The Challenge

The single most critical problem in our world today is captured in the word "alienation." In all of human history it has been so. At this writing, dozens of wars—large and small—are raging around the globe. An average of twenty-four disasters, some natural and some caused (like the 400,000 Rwandans slaughtered in six weeks during the spring of 1994), are taxing the humanitarian resources of the international community. Nation against nation, tribe against tribe, family against family, sibling against sibling, parent against child, child against parent. It hints at the apocalyptic.

In every arena of society, leaders are being called to show followers how to find their way through the morass of ancient rivalries, prejudices, greed, and self-centeredness. But answers do not come simply. Presidents and prime ministers have worked and continue to work with diligence. Diplomats crisscross the globe daily. Community service volunteers organize foot patrols in neighborhoods and crisis counseling for children whose classmates have been killed on the playground. We all know where it starts, of course. Problems do not begin with nations. They begin in individuals and spread to families, tribes, and nations. Then the question becomes "How do *I* deal with the individuals *I* lead at home, work, or the larger community? How do love, leadership, and power come together in *me?*

The Task

When we ask the question: "What is a leader's task?" the answer would probably be something like "To achieve the stated mission of the leader and the group." That takes at least two things: the *training* and the *equipping* of the followers to execute that mission. Studies in management and leadership have shown again and again that it is not the technical or mechanical side of leadership that is hard to convey, but the conceptual side.

Definition of words is always an issue in this kind of discussion. Some words like *elephant* have the same meaning everywhere. But when we move from the objective arena to the subjective, all bets are off. Historical intent modified by usage invariably affects words and meanings.

For example, in any culture *leadership* means *power. Power* almost always means control over others. *Love,* on the other hand, has a great range of definitions around the world, and its significance in the culture varies greatly from place to place. In modern Western culture, *love* is most often characterized in romantic, self-centered terms.

Jesus portrayed leadership in terms of power too. But His power is turned inward in self-control. Unlike trying to control others, which drains energy, self-control generates energy for service. Loving acts are the result. Love becomes practical and other-oriented, reflecting the definition already suggested: "Love is the accurate estimate and the adequate supply of another person's need."

So if the key challenge for leaders is dealing with alienation among people in order to progress, then the leaders' power must be used in a way that doesn't alienate. They must deal with themselves realistically, because the leaders I know really like to lead and are gifted to do so. They enjoy power and often use it well. The tendency, however, is to lean on positional, economic, and informational power as opposed to relational power. Relational power takes so much longer to develop.

Relational power is inherently a shared commodity. It takes an investment of time and a considerable amount of risk to see it take shape. On the surface, that should not intimidate a leader because that's part of him or her. According to Haas, "having permission to express oneself, combined with the willingness to take risks are the essential elements . . . of leadership."

If that statement is true, and I believe it is, a revolution could happen. As a matter of course, the significant leaders I know take risks with their careers, programs, and sometimes with their enterprises. Certainly, what most might see as barriers, they see as opportunities. With that in mind, the real risk comes into view.

What about taking a risk with my person? It is not in the sense of being point person for a squad of soldiers in battle, though that's certainly the role of a leader. Rather, it is by opening myself to another for the purpose of sharing love and power. It is an act that bears directly on effectiveness.

At first glance that idea is problematic because American individualism is a part of our national fabric. John Wayne and Rocky are our prototype heroes, but even they can't win alone.

Leadership that Goes Beyond
We live in a world that has its own view of love, power, and leadership. Folks need love, want their share of pow-

er, and aren't all that trusting of leaders. Yet leaders still need to lead. How do they do it? Not alone.

The original biblical injunction that "It is not good for man to be alone" applies to leaders also. As a matter of fact, it may be needed there most of all.

As a twenty-five-year-old pastor, I came to appreciate that dynamic early on. My friend, Paul McGarvey, was older than I by fifteen years. He was not of the clergy. He was a football coach. But he could understand my fears and my dreams. He took the time to listen to and discuss my issues. Virtually any time of the day and night, he was available to me.

Paul did not just spend time, he invested time. The things that began to grow inside me in those years—the attitudes and perspectives—have remained.

He did not only enter my life and my world, he invited me into his. When that happened, I understood better the idea of hospitality. In Eugene Peterson's paraphrase of the New Testament, *The Message*, he expresses Paul's instructions to Timothy in a marvelous way:

> A leader must be well-thought-of, committed to his wife, cool and collected, accessible, and hospitable. He must know what he's talking about, not be overfond of wine, not pushy but gentle, not thin-skinned, not money-hungry. He must handle his own affairs well, attentive to his own children and having their respect (1 Tim. 3:2-3).

It's most interesting that self-control is the motif of this passage, and the specific issues are women, wine, temper, money, and children. Why then, right in the middle of his discourse, does he throw in *hospitality*? Obviously, this isn't cookie and punch time. What's going on here? At the center of his thesis on personal control, he introduces the idea of "the open heart." Hospitality says, "Come to my place. Share my life. We can be and do more together than apart."

Hospitality is at the core of a leadership model. It is God's character. To open oneself, to invite another person in, is terribly risky, especially in the competitive world of leaders. It's not safe for a variety of reasons, but they are not bad reasons. By inviting another leader into my life, I create a dynamic—a synergy—that shakes the foundations of tradition. It pours new wine into brittle old wineskins. A small group of leaders encouraging one another and acting together can be very dangerous indeed, because their joint influence is so great. One person may symbolize the effort of the group, but no one stands alone.

In Jesus' darkest hour at Gethsemane, He asked His disciples to be with Him. As God, He may have needed nothing, but as a man, He needed His friends. That's not a statement about weakness, but about strength. It says, "We can be more and do more together."

The phone rang in our home. I answered and heard an Eastern European-accented voice. The gentleman identified himself as an ambassador. He was responding to an invitation to meet with a few other diplomats and politicians in a small leadership group. The purpose was simply to be together around Christ and have an opportunity to share individual needs and dreams. Hopefully, they would learn to make themselves available to one another beyond the day-to-day commonality of their particular roles. They would come to understand that the highest level of leadership—to be effective—demands the deepest commitments to a few close people. In that experience, they would find solace, protection, joy, and direction.

Years ago at the college, I had a trustee friend, a lumberman who was full of sayings, stories, and maxims. After my first couple of years at the school, when the honeymoon was over and the challenges were mounting, he told me, "The problem with shinnying up the flagpole, Dick, is that the higher you go the better chance you have of getting shot in the backside!" In his own practical and earthy way, he had stated the problem that every leader in any public venue has experienced. Whoever said, "It's lonely at the top" had been there.

Given that fact, when a person in a place of corporate or public responsibility takes the opportunity to have a friend who keeps confidences and wants nothing but to serve, amazing things can happen. "Friend" is one of the most powerful words in the world. It speaks to commitment and time and a discretionary choice. It has an intentionality about it that is full of latent power.

In the spring of 1993, I sat in Washington, D.C. with a new colleague and a senior foreign diplomat—a man of significant tenure and some prestige in the diplomatic community. As I listened, their conversation wandered through official duties, current events, and then turned to matters of personal concern for the ambassador—family matters.

There was no probing or pressing, only gentle and sincere inquiry on particular matters, which obviously had been discussed on prior occasions. The diplomat thanked him for his concern and friendship.

Then, unexpectedly, this Oxford-educated gentleman turned to me, pointed to my friend, and said, "Dick, did you know that this is the most powerful person in Washington?"

I replied, "No, Mr. Ambassador, I didn't. Why would you say that?"

Softly, he replied, "Because this is a town that operates on relationships. Who you know counts for everything. And this man has more friends than anyone else in this city!"

For weeks afterward, I reflected on that statement. On the basis of subsequent experiences in the capital, I believe that the ambassador was essentially right.

Within the friendship of two or three comes affirmation, accountability, and security. Strength is the product of that interaction. Stances can be maintained. Actions can be initiated. Clarity of thinking and boldness in the face of threat become hallmarks of such commitments.

Paul had his *company*. At the close of a letter to his

spiritual son, Timothy, he gave a glimpse, in a kind of poignant way, of his interdependence with them:

Do your best to come to me quickly, for Demas, because he loved this world, has deserted me and has gone to Thessalonica. Crescens has gone to Galatia, and Titus to Dalmatia. Only Luke is with me. Get Mark and bring him with you, because he is helpful to me in my ministry. I sent Tychicus to Ephesus (2 Tim. 4:9-12).

Jesus needed and asked for the prayers and support of His disciples as He entered Gethsemane. Then when they fell asleep, He called on the only resource left, His Father. Communion with His Father sustained Jesus all the way to the cross—the instrument of death the Romans employed to deal with those persons they couldn't agree with or contain.

A student leadership forum gave me further insight into the power of leadership coalitions. The congressional representative from Kansas had been master of ceremonies for three days at the Hyatt Regency Hotel. Four blocks from Capitol Hill, leadership groups from the House and the Senate hosted 500 university students. The purpose was to encourage young people that faith and values had critical meaning in the political/economic life of our country and that when leaders really liked one another, power took on a whole new dimension.

It had been a very moving time. At the last plenary session, the representative said, "I have not had the opportunity to challenge you as a speaker this year, so I'd like to say this one thing before I close out my responsibilities. You have heard many things in your university classes, but there is one thing that you will not hear in management, political science, or history. That is this: Jesus Christ is the greatest leader that ever lived. And don't ever forget it!"

The ballroom erupted in thunderous applause. Even in those few short days, the students had seen what could happen if men and women in power chose to follow

Christ, put aside differences on issues, and simply become a group of friends trying to nurture the next generation of leaders. Again, the giants had lain down.

It was much more than just being acquaintances. Those people seemed to authentically like one another. Most of them met in one forum or another every week to talk together, to pray for one another, and to ask for help in meeting the incredible challenges of the nation and more specifically in their own states or districts. They had found that to open themselves to a peer—even a member of the opposing political party—was not to be weakened or demeaned but to be elevated.

Many of these congressional participants carried enormous political clout. They had reputations to make and protect. But they had stumbled onto the mystery—the mystery that, when explored, had power and peace at its core.

They knew all about coalitions, alliances, and strange political bedfellows born out of political pragmatism. These friendships had nothing to do with that kind of expediency. The depth and vitality of brotherhood and sisterhood based in the reconciling Spirit of Christ left politics in the dust.

The effect on the student leaders at that conference was quite real. When power kneels in humility, it ultimately stands taller. When position intentionally releases its grasp, reconciliation becomes a possibility. Where walls are reformed into bridges, people can see and meet one another in new ways.

When a group of leaders loves one another, they model something that goes light years beyond words or actions by the individuals. They set the stage for the healing of the nations. If leaders could learn to risk themselves with one another, not just their ideas or projects, it would create a following that could change an entire society.

The most recent literature on leadership indicates that leaders of great companies all love what they do. They love their work. I submit that loving the followers takes leadership one level deeper. Indeed, loving people is the basis for powerful leadership. In addition, a leadership team loving one another creates a model that encourages security and hope among those who watch.

When our four children were small, they illustrated this idea in a cute way. Ruth was at the kitchen sink one day, and I sneaked up behind her, encircled her waist with my arms, and drew her back to me. She laughingly mocked a struggle, saying, "Not now, Dick!"

Finally, she turned, put soapy arms around my neck, and gave me a hug. Almost instantly we felt little hands down by our knees. Looking down, we saw four little faces grinning up at us.

At first, I thought the kids were trying to pry us apart. And then the real reason for their interruption dawned on me. They wanted a piece of the action. They had apparently been in the living room. Hearing giggles in the kitchen, one of them had stuck her head around the corner. Seeing what was happening, she had no doubt whispered, "Hey, the Giants are doing that again!" And they came running.

People loving each other is magnetic. It draws a crowd. The activity alone reflects the spirit in which Christ came to Bethlehem, and that's very attractive. He said it this way: "If I be lifted up, I'll draw all men to Me." And it works. It works because it's right. The leaders I know like things that work—and are right.

It's also risky business, but that's OK. Leaders love risks. They're used to rocking the boat. Now they can try stepping out of it!

The Final Point

In the marketplaces of our lives, amid the calls for attention and the viewing of wares, we have a goal to pursue: relationships that bind us together and give us power at one and the same time.

We are designed for relationship, and we are called to create a climate in which relationships can flourish in whatever leadership capacity we find ourselves.

It is in that climate that persons, young and old, become secure and stable.

It is in that climate that the frightened find safety and the arrogant find humility.

It is in that climate that the weak are made strong and the strong are made tender.

It is in that climate that vulnerability is shown to be a virtue and power becomes a shared commodity.

It is in that climate that we find trust and hope and love.

It is in that climate that we discover what we are really made for.

And it all begins when the Giant lies down.

WHEN THE GIANT LIES DOWN

The guide instructs us carefully,
to be in groups of two or three;
but—willful, independent me,
I choose to walk alone.
So much easier, I think,
to do it on my own.

There'll be . . .
no annoying confrontations,
no obligating dependence,
no second opinions,
no risky relationships,
to slow me down.

Instead, I find . . .
no honest challenges,
no wholesome trust,
no wise alternatives,
no enriching friendships,
to grow me up.

—Ruth Foth

Chapter 11

One Last Look

The first hint of California spring touched the branches of the peach and almond trees in the central valley. The sky was a warming blue. The air was crisp but edging toward cool.

Fifty cars, led by a steel-gray hearse, moved at moderate speed down the country road bordered by orchards, vineyards, and an occasional house. Approaching a modest, ranch-style home on his right, the driver slowed perceptibly.

It was the home of Roy Blakeley, patriarch of a clan consisting of his wife, Opal, five children and spouses, twenty-two grandchildren, and two great-grandchildren. His death had brought them home from across America. They joined 150 other members of the extended family in a private memorial service, with a much larger public service to follow the next day

As a pastor, he had been a community leader for fifty-four years. He was a pastor with the heart of a farmer—a planter, grower, harvester, and fixer.

The planter pioneered churches, schools, a senior citizens' village, and international missions projects, along with Vietnamese and Russian resettlement efforts in America. The grower always nurtured and encouraged, first his immediate family and second dozens of friends. The harvester helped hundreds of people, young and old, embark on the journey of learning to love God and one another.

But the thing that made him unique was his penchant for finding and fixing things. The most precise word would be "salvage."

A tenderhearted genius. What others saw as junk, he saw as joy. What another discarded as trash, he claimed in triumph. The rejected things, he redeemed.

He was the consummate loving leader who could not settle for taking plenty and making it more, but took little and made it grand. He did that one person at a time. That's why so many loved him back.

The hearse slowed with intention, a flag dipping in honor of a fallen soldier. As it did, the horns of the two cars immediately behind, carrying the thirteen grandsons, his pallbearers, began to honk. Then arms exploded out the open windows waving old caps—old soiled baseball-style caps, each with a different logo and story. All Grandad's. They were mostly given to him by friends, companies, local businesses, and schools. The boys had worn them in his memory. Each choosing and keeping his favorite, at Grandma's insistence.

Only minutes before, we had been overwhelmed with emotion watching the older boys gently carry the simple poplar casket out of the church. The younger boys followed in a double line, walking tall, each wearing one of Grandad's caps.

Suddenly, all up and down the procession, horns began to honk. Windows came down. Sunroofs slid back. Arms appeared, waving handkerchiefs. Cheers ricocheted through the orchards. Tears began to flow again. It was the Fourth of July and Christmas and Easter on Carver Road. As the cortege turned the corner toward the cemetery, one observer said, "The roar was so loud it sounded like a train coming down the road!" Grandad would've gotten a kick out of it.

Roy Blakeley did not lead by intimidation. Nor did he brandish the authority of his several offices. He simply loved and nurtured people, those closest to him first. He knew that the individual and the family were the core of a powerful society. And in the end, loving God and one another was the foundation upon which the right things got done.

He had discovered early in life that relationship was the heart of leadership. Nothing else carried such power. Nothing else allowed anybody and everybody to bring something to the table. Nothing else could salvage lives and careers and families. Nothing else could last.

Of all the kinds of people Roy touched in his three-quarters of a century, none would be more important to him than the children. Several generations of kids, now adults, remember him on his knees hugging them in the church breezeway. They are recounting to *their* children, no doubt even as we write, the funny-stories-with-a-punchline of *Herman the Horse* and *The Royal Pig*. The children knew they had access. They could touch him. They could share his power. He was a giant, but they knew he was *for* them.

They didn't know it, but every time they were with him, they were visiting Bethlehem. The very notion of a giant-of-a-God-out-there-somewhere, whom we don't and can't comprehend, is unnerving. And the idea that the Giant might come to us in a vulnerable, touchable way doesn't make sense from our own experiences with most human leaders.

But when a human leader—mother, father, teacher, CEO, grandparent, sibling, friend—humbles himself or herself, understanding that real power is in relationship, unbelievable things can happen. Warmth, knowledge, vision, redemption, reconciliation, trust, hope, reality. It all comes together. It all begins when the Giant lies down.

As we stood by Father Blakeley's grave with the early spring breeze tugging at coattails and dresses, the feeling was strong. Plenty of grief, to be sure, with the memory of at least six grandsons over six feet each, standing and kneeling by his casket in private moments, laying their large hands upon that still chest, and weeping for their loss. But the strongest sense that afternoon was one of gratitude for a life lived fully and well. Intensely and humbly. A model of strength and kindness. Love, leadership, and power in a work shirt, jeans, and a soiled cap.

Walking back to the car, I mused on his natural optimism, his get-after-it attitude, and his consistent sense that God wanted to do some good things with us every day.

The early morning phone calls used to capture all those things for me. I was twenty-three, fresh out of graduate school, and ready to change the world with my acquired prowess when Father Blakeley took me on as his associate.

I had asked him what he wanted me to do, and he would give me all the room in the world to initiate and grow by saying, "Just go build the kingdom, Dick. We need lots of help. You'll do fine."

But the 6 A.M. phone calls became legend. His melodious, rather husky voice would sound in my ear: "Hey, Foth! Did you hear what happened?"

Invariably drawn in, I'd struggle to sound as if I'd been up for an hour already. "No. What?" I'd reply.

The enthusiasm I'd first heard him project when I met him at kids' camp a dozen years before came through, as he'd chuckle: "The sun came up again today. It's beautiful. Look outside and see what I see." Then he'd invite me down to his house for a breakfast of pancakes, eggs, and steaming coffee.

The morning after he died, I awoke with a start about 6 A.M. Every sense was alert, trying to figure out what had brought me out of a sound sleep.

And then suddenly I knew. I was waiting for the phone to ring. Waiting for that voice to say, "Hey, Foth. Did you hear what happened? The sun came up again today!"